Dedicated to Savy and Peanut, who make every day an adventure. Thank you for traveling the world with us.

ANTARCTICA

Educational Resources, Crafts & Activities for Kids

Sarah M. Prowant, MSN-Ed, RN

Savy Activities
Colorado, USA

Savy Activities© All Rights Reserved

TERMS & CONDITIONS

This product is licensed for single use only (single home or classroom). Redistributing, selling, editing or sharing any part of this product in any part thereof is strictly forbidden without the written permission of Savy Activities. You may make copies for your personal use but will need to purchase separate licenses for use in additional classrooms and/or schools. Failure to comply is a legal copyright infringement and will be prosecuted to the full extent of the law.

When posting photos of any part of this product on social media, please give credit to "Savy Activities" by hyperlinking to our website and tagging us as @SavyActivities on social media.

We reserve the right to change this policy at any time. If you have any questions regarding this or other of our materials, please contact us directly.

FOR BEST RESULTS:

 When assembling a 3D model, glue a second piece of thick paper with a craft glue stick to back of each sheet of model pieces (prior to cutting pieces) to provide additional stability when assembled.

 Laminate all cards & posters with at least 3 ml lamination for additional protection.

 If printing from an ebook, cardstock paper (>60 lbs) provides best results for cards, models and manipulative activities, while standard printer paper is adequate for recipes, lessons, etc. Please set printer to "FIT TO PAGE" when printing for best results.

FOLLOW US ON SOCIAL MEDIA!

 @savyactivities

 /SavyActivities

www.SavyActivities.com

WHATS INCLUDED:

- Antarctica Info Poster, Flag & History Timeline
- Fun Facts & Treaty Poster
- Antarctica Stations Pinning & Map
- Principles of Daylight Poster, Experiment
- Sungraph Slider
- Sailing Ship Craft & Classification Poster
- Heroic Age Antarctic Expeditions Cards
- Vintage Snow Goggles Craft
- Antarctic Explorers Standup Cutouts
- Vintage Polar Gear Poster
- The Polar Race Mini-Book
- Snow Travel Experiment
- Banjo Craft
- Checkers Game
- A Trip to Antarctica
- Hoosh Recipe
- Penguin Post Office Model
- Design a Postage Stamp & Poster
- Penguin Species Cards & Habitat Zones
- Units of Measurement - Penguins
- Anatomy & Life Cycle of the Emperor Penguin
- Rockhopper Penguin Felt Puzzle
- Penguin Counting
- Penguin Egg Waddle
- North Vs. South Pole Venn Diagram
- Arctic Desert Habitat Match
- Antarctic Animal Finger Puppets
- Paper Bag Fur Seal Puppet
- Blubber Experiment
- Glacier Melt Experiment
- Types of Glaciers Cards
- Snowflake Formation & Matching
- Paper Snowflakes & Cursive Tracing
- Salt Snowflakes Craft

Antarctica

National Flora: Antarctic Starwort
National Fauna: Penguin
Distinctive Location: South Pole
Currency: None
Language: Varied
National Holiday(s):
Antarctica Day - December 1
Midwinter Day - June 21
Famous Landmarks:
Deception Island
Paradise Bay
Ross Ice Shelf
Mount Erebus
Vinson Massif
Paulet Island
Cape Renard
Lake Vostok
Onyx River
Blood Falls

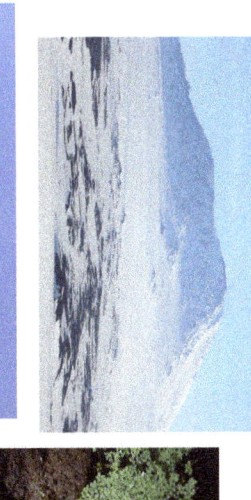

Antarctica

Antarctica

Antarctica Fun Facts

Antarctica has two active volcanoes, Mount Erebus and Deception Island volcanic caldera.

Scientists claim that if the West Antarctic Ice Sheet melted, it would raise global sea levels by 16 ft.

There is no time zones in Antarctica, as the lines of longitude or time zones around the globe, all meet at a single point.

Antarctica is, on average, the windiest place on earth, with reported wind speeds up to 200 mph.

The Dry Valleys in Antarctica are the driest places on earth, preventing even snow and ice accumulation.

Antarctica is a desert, because it receives very little precipitation.

The Antarctic Treaty is an international agreement to govern the continent together as a reserve for peace and science.

Antarctica holds most of the world's fresh water, about 90% locked in a vast ice sheet.

Antarctica Fun Facts

Antarctica has one of the world's largest mountain ranges, the *Gamburtsev Mountains*, but is buried completely by snow and ice.

There are 30 different countries that operate 80 research stations situated around the continent.

Deep Lake in Antarctica is so salty that it cannot freeze, even as low as -15° Celsius!

In 1978, Emilio Marco Palma became the first human birth on Antarctica.

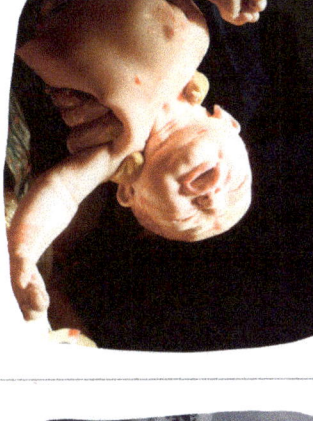

Taylor Glacier or "Blood Falls" has high levels of iron in the water, which rusts and gives it its amazing red color.

Because of the earth's tilt, the sun does not rise in Antarctica throughout the entire winter season.

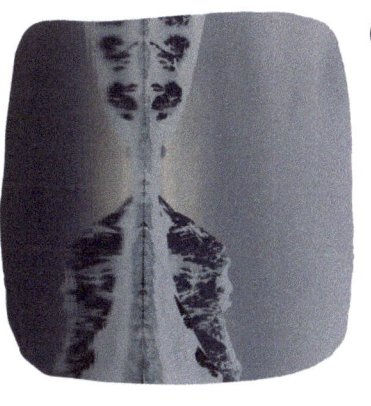

Antarctica has eight churches throughout the various research stations of Antarctica.

Tiny nematode worms are the most common land animal in Antarctica.

Antarctica Stations

Scott Base
New Zealand

Brown Station
Argentina

General Bernardo O'Higgins
Chili

Bellingshausen Station
Russia

Brown Station

Established: April 6, 1951
Country: Argentina
Location: Sanavirón Peninsula (Paradise Harbor), Danco Coast
Operation: Summer

Brown Station is one of the most complete biology laboratories on the Antarctic Peninsula, and includes a main house of 3,140 square feet, two 7,900 gallon fuel tanks and an additional building exclusive for scientific research, equipped with three labs, photography workshop, emergency radio station, office and library.

Scott Base

Established: January 20, 1957
Country: New Zealand
Location: Pram Point on Ross Island, near Mount Erebus
Operation: Year-round

Scott Base is a collection of green buildings linked by all-weather corridors, which can accommodate 85 people in summer, and 10-14 people in winter. The base was designed to research earth sciences, but today conducts research in many fields. In 1985 scientific diving operations began, completing over 1,200 dives to date.

Bellingshausen Station

Established: 1968
Country: Russia
Location: Collins Harbour, on King George Island (South Shetland Islands)
Operation: Year-round

Bellingshausen Station is also the location of Trinity Church, the only permanently staffed Eastern Orthodox church in Antarctica. The Antarctic Peninsula are considered to have the mildest living conditions in Antarctica, and is also one of the few locations in Antarctica classified as a tundra rather than an ice cap climate.

General Bernardo O'Higgins

Established: February 18, 1948
Country: Chile
Location: North Antarctic Peninsula, Cape Legoupil
Operation: Year-round

Base General Bernardo O'Higgins Riquelme is a satellite ground station to collect data from satellite-based sensors in the south pole. High bandwidth sensors generate too much data to be stored on board the satellite for transmission to ground stations elsewhere. This base has a borderline polar tundra climate that is extremely close to a polar ice cap climate.

Antarctica Stations

Vernadsky Research Base
Ukraine

Port Lockroy
Great Britain

Davis Station
Australia

Neumayer Station 3
Germany

Port Lockroy

Established: February 11, 1944
Country: Great Britain
Location: NW Wiencke Island, Antarctic Peninsula.
Operation: Year-round

Port Lockroy was established as a research station between 1944 to 1962. It is known for being one of the first to measure the ionosphere, and the first recording of an atmospheric whistler (electronic waves), from Antarctica. In 1996, it was renovated and is now a museum and post office operated by the United Kingdom, and one of the most popular tourist destinations.

Vernadsky Research Base

Established: 1947
Country: Ukraine
Location: Marina Point on Galindez Island (Argentine Islands), near Kiev Peninsula.
Operation: Year-round

Vernadsky Research Base consists of nine buildings standing on rock foundations, and studies meteorology, upper atmospheric physics, geomagnetism, ozone, seismology, glaciology, ecology, biology and physiology research. Located in a marine sub-Antarctic climate, it has also studied long-term temperature trends that indicate global warming.

Neumayer Station 3

Established: February 20, 2009
Country: Germany
Location: Ekström Ice Shelf south of Neumayer-Station II.
Operation: Year-round

Neumayer-Station III was built on dry ice-cap terrain which moves approximately 200 meters per year towards the open sea, with an expected lifespan of 25 to 30 years. This and previous Neumayer stations have researched meteorology, geophysics and atmospheric chemistry, and more recently infrasound and marine acoustics.

Davis Station

Established: January 13, 1957
Country: Australia
Location: Antarctic oasis (Vestfold Hills).
Operation: Year-round

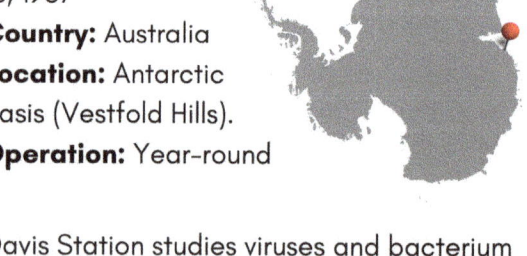

Davis Station studies viruses and bacterium using molecular genetic techniques in glacial lakes, the impact of environmental change and pollution on Antarctic marine ecosystems, atmospheric research, algae growth, the impact of climate change, and the study of the Law Dome, the bedrock geology and structure of the East Antarctic ice sheet.

Antarctica Stations

McMurdo Station
United States

Great Wall Station
China

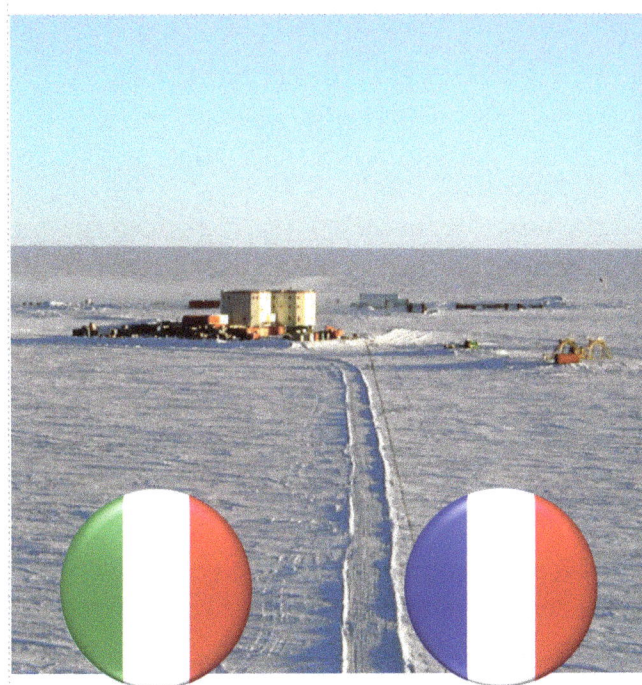

Concordia
Italy/France

Maitri
India

Great Wall Station

Established: February 20, 1985
Country: China
Location: Fildes Peninsula, King George Island.
Operation: Year-round

The Great Wall Station is built on ice-free rock, about 33 feet above sea level. It is also the first Chinese research station in Antarctica. Located near a nature reserve where groups of penguins and seals are often seen, this station has around 25 buildings with state of the art communication facilities and scientific laboratories.

McMurdo Station

Established: February 16, 1956
Country: United States
Location: Southern Ross Island, McMurdo Sound.
Operation: Year-round

McMurdo Station is the largest community in Antarctica (housing over a thousand residents at times) located in a polar ice cap climate. This base features a science station, harbor, three airfields, heliport and more than 100 buildings along with the continents two ATMs. This station focuses on scientific studies, including a comprehensive diving program with a hyperbaric chamber.

Maitri

Established: January, 1989
Country: India
Location: Schirmacher Oasis.
Operation: Year-round

Maitri, also known as Friendship Research Center is India's second permanent research facility and includes modern facilities dedicated to researching biology, earth sciences, glaciology, atmospheric sciences, meteorology, cold region engineering, communication, human physiology, and medicine. Freshwater is provided through a freshwater lake named Lake Priyadarshini, in front of Maitri.

Concordia Research Station

Established: 2005
Country: France/Italy
Location: Dome C, Antarctic Plateau.
Operation: Year-round

Concordia Station is one of the coldest bases with harsh living conditions including isolation, prolonged darkness and high altitudes. This environment promotes the study of chronic hypobaric hypoxia, stress secondary to confinement and isolation, circadian rhythm, sleep disruption, psychology, telemedicine, and astrobiology. In addition, Concordia Station also provides extremely accurate astronomical observations.

Antarctica Stations

Amundsen-Scott South Pole Station
United States

SANAE IV Station
South Africa

Vostok Station
Russia

Showa Station
Japan

SANAE IV Station

Established: 1997
Country: South Africa
Location: Vesleskarvet Queen Maud Land Antarctica.
Operation: Year-round

This station is built on top of a distinctive flat-topped nunatak, Vesleskarvet. The structure stands on stilts, allowing snow to blow through underneath. SANAE provides research in diverse fields such as oceanography, biology, geology and geomorphology. Recent projects have also focused on sources of renewable energy such as solar and wind power generation.

Amundsen-Scott South Pole Station

Established: November 1956
Country: United States
Location: Geographic South Pole, Antarctic Plateau
Operation: Year-round

Originally built to study the geophysics of the polar regions of Earth, this station has been continuously occupied since it was built, rebuilt, expanded, and upgraded several times. Before 1956, there was no permanent artificial structure at the pole. The winter darkness and dry atmosphere make the station an excellent site for astronomical observations.

Showa Station

Established: 1957
Country: Japan
Location: East Ongul Island, Queen Maud Land
Operation: Year-round

Showa Station provides research on astronomy, meteorology, biology and earth sciences. It has over 60 separate buildings, including an administration building, living quarters, power plant, sewage treatment facility, science buildings, observatory, satellite and incinerator. It also includes a heliport for transportation.

Vostok Station

Established: December 16, 1957
Country: Russia
Location: Princess Elizabeth Land
Operation: Year-round

Vostok Station has an ice cap climate, with subzero temperatures year round. Annual precipitation (snow) of only 22 millimeters (0.87 inches), making it one of the driest places on Earth. Research includes ice core drilling and magnetometry. Ice core samples have been used to study past environmental conditions over previous glacial periods.

Antarctica

Antarctica

*Please note that the locations may not be exact as markers are positioned for best visual fit.

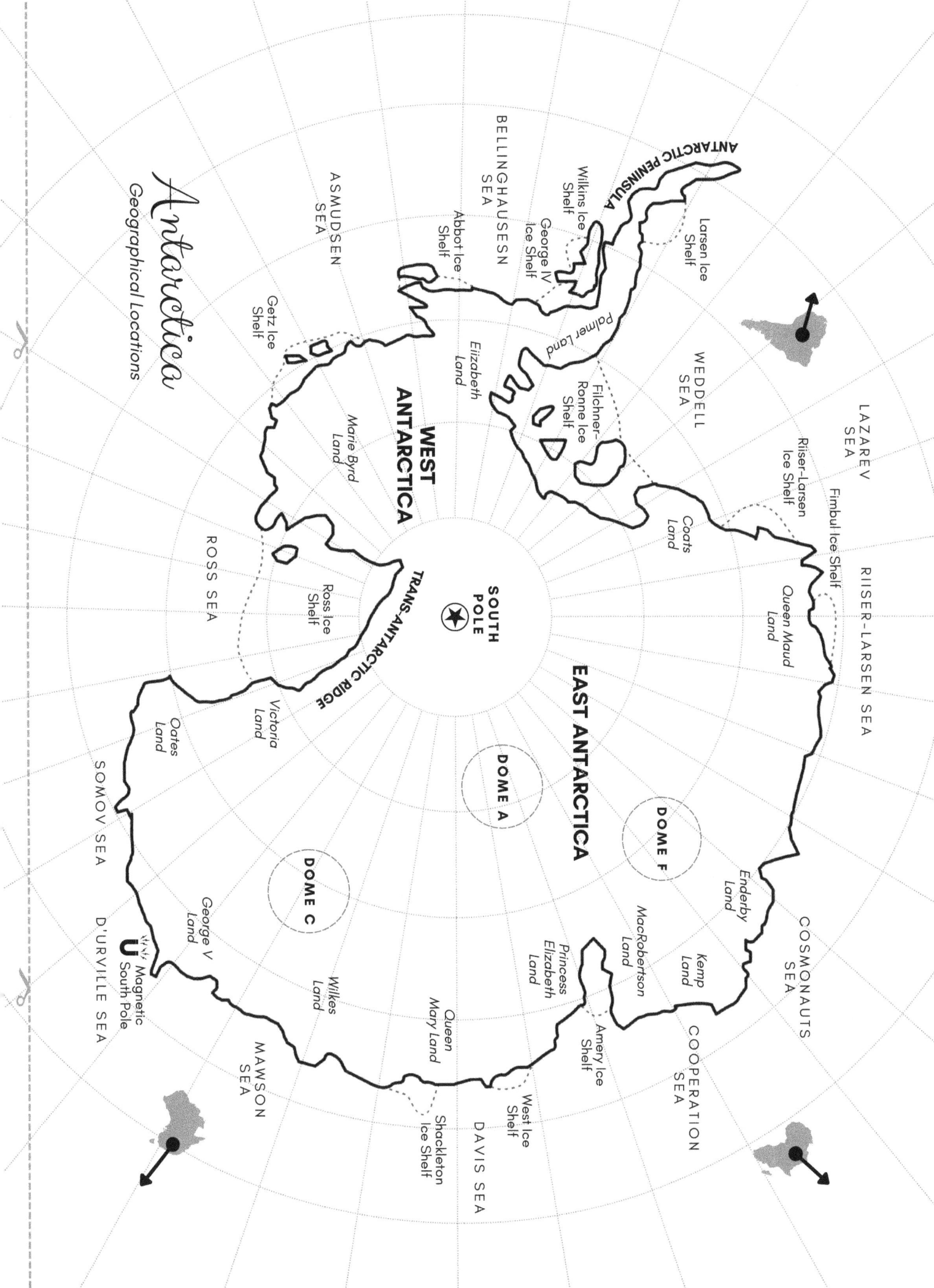

Principles of Daylight

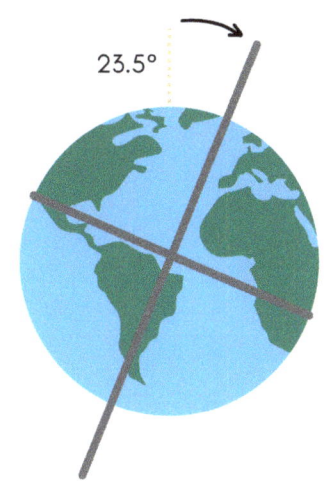

The earth rotates on a central axis which is angled at 23.5° – this allows some areas of the earth to get more sunlight than others, depending on the rotation of the earth.

The earth also rotates around the sun. As it rotates on its axis to complete a day, it also orbits around the sun to complete a year cycle. At some points in the Earth's orbit around the Sun, the tilt causes one hemisphere to lean toward the Sun while the other one is tilted away, especially at areas closer to the poles.

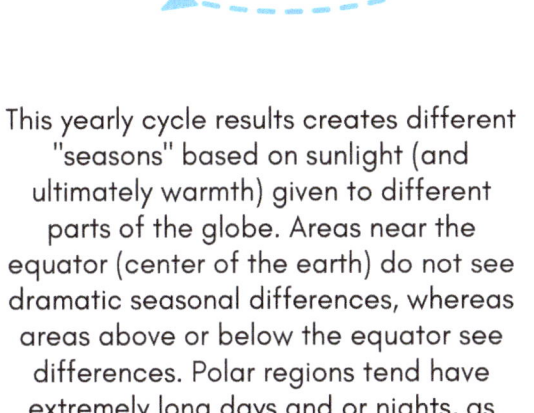

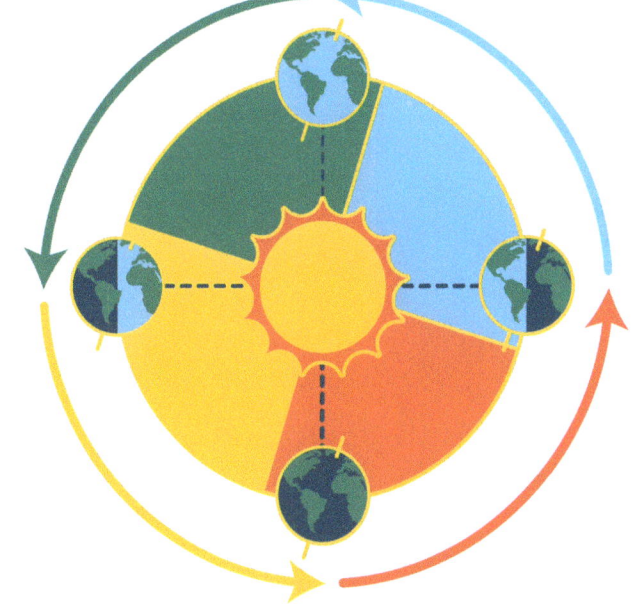

This yearly cycle results creates different "seasons" based on sunlight (and ultimately warmth) given to different parts of the globe. Areas near the equator (center of the earth) do not see dramatic seasonal differences, whereas areas above or below the equator see differences. Polar regions tend have extremely long days and or nights, as these locations can go months without sunlight or sunset.

FLASHLIGHT DAYLIGHT EXPERIMENT

Materials
- 3-4-inch Styrofoam Ball
- Scissors
- Craft Glue
- Flashlight

Instructions

Due to the tilt of the earth (23.5°) each side of the earth does not receive the same amount of sunlight as it revolves on it's axis. In fact, areas farther away from the equator (center) receive more or less total sunlight hours in a day and less direct solar rays, creating a colder environment.

   Cut out included continents. Glue onto ball in approximate geographical locations. **Note:** Continent illustrations are not to size, and are only to provide estimated locations for this activity. Allow to dry completely. Place "sun" outline over flashlight to create a sun. Find a dark area and shine the light onto the ball. Observe what continents are illuminated and which ones are "darker" or having night. Compare this with time zones in other countries. For instance, when it's noon in Brazil, what time is it in Japan? Does this correlate with the "sunlight" from the flashlight? Compare other countries/continents.

SUNGRAPH SLIDER

Instructions

Because the earth rotates at a tilt, different latitudes receive more or less sun, depending on the time of year as the earth orbits the sun. Areas near the equator tend to receive about the same sunlight year round, while areas north or south receive more sun during one half of the year and less during the other. At the poles this is so extreme that the area receives six months of polar day and six months of polar night.

Materials
- Sungraph Templates
- Scissors
- Craft Glue
- Craft Knife

Cut out included sungraphs and slider. Cut out display window in slider and fold in half, as indicated along dashed lines. Glue the top edge together with craft glue, making sure there is still plenty of space for the graphs to slide back and forth. Allow to dry completely. Pull sunscapes back and forth in slider, observing the average sunlight hours of the different locations. Compare to other locations - how do they differ? **Note:** sunscapes do not adjust for daylight savings time and are only estimates of average daylight hours.

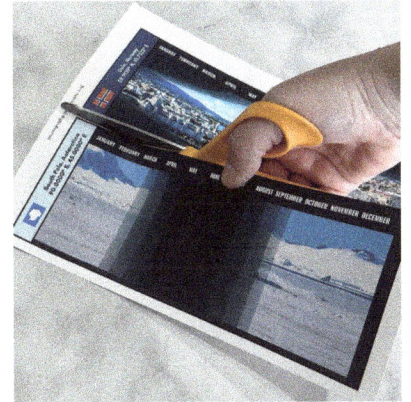
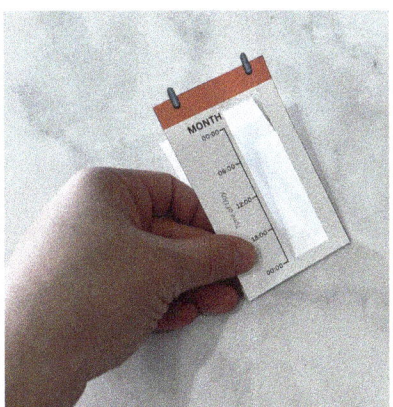
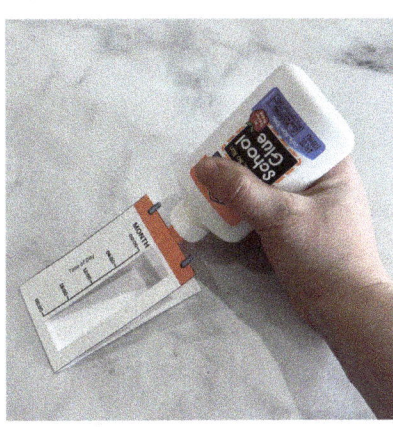

Sungraphs

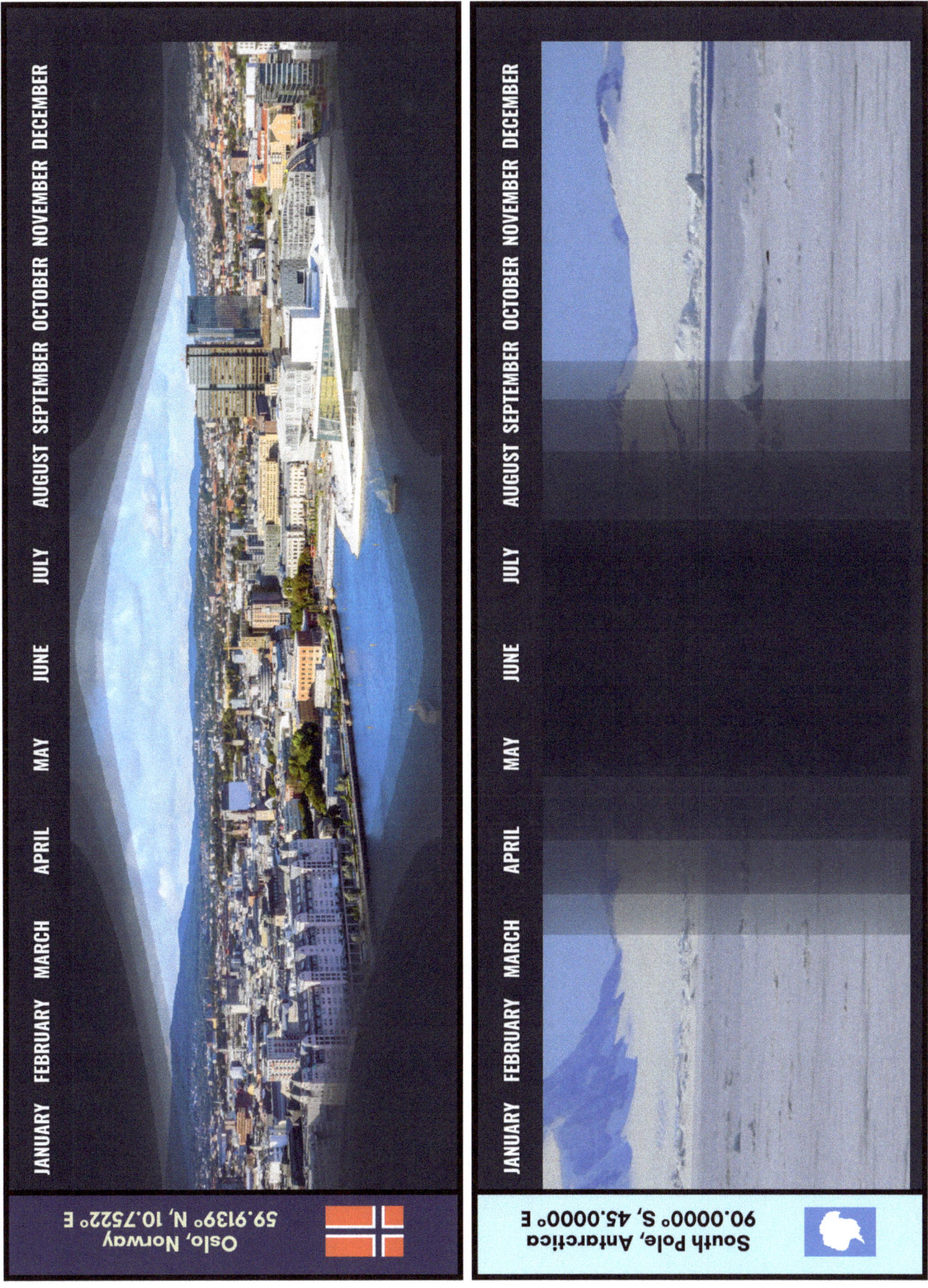

Sungraphs

Sungraphs

Sungraph Slider

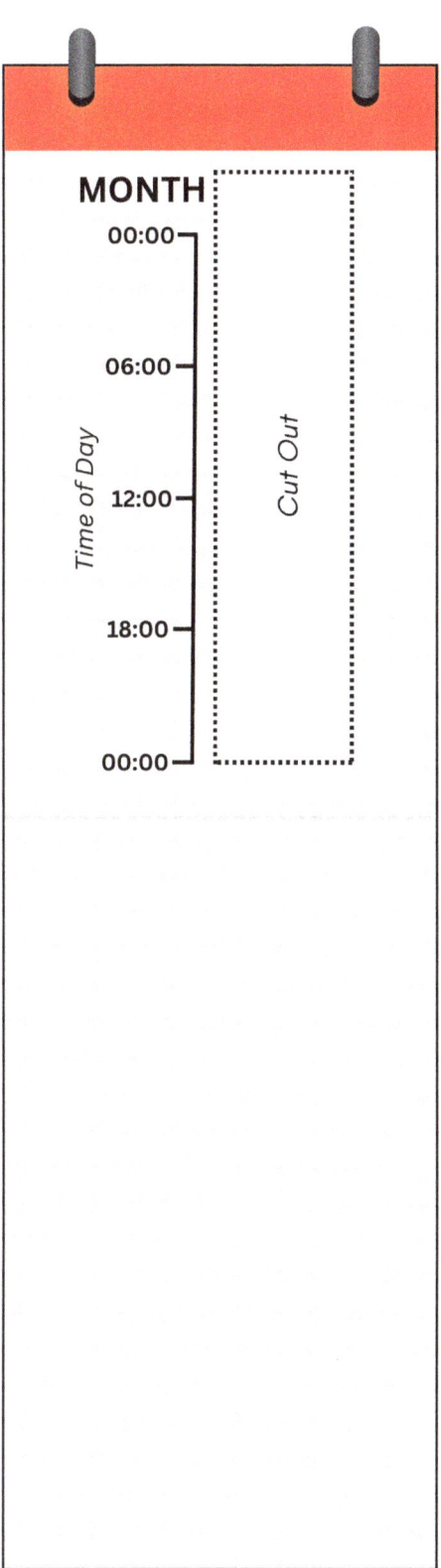

Ship Hull Template

SAILING SHIP CRAFT

Instructions

During the Heroic Age, expeditions to the Antarctic used ships which navigated the icy waters of the southern polar region and ultimately the continent of Antarctica. Sailing vessels are often classified by their rigging, which includes the masts or sails used as well as accompanied ropes or cables. The most common ships used were barque, barquentine and schooner rig configurations.

Materials
- Ship Hull Template
- Scissors
- Construction Paper
- Craft Glue
- Skewer Sticks

Trace the included ship hull template onto dark colored paper. Cut out outline and glue onto a contrasting color background. Allow to dry. Cut up to 4-5 skewer sticks (Most sailing vessels have less than five or less mast poles) to fit between the top of the hull and the top of the paper. Use craft glue to secure in place. Allow to dry completely. Cut out masts from light colored paper. While most mast shapes tend to be triangular or square, be creative if desired. **Discuss:** compare finished design with sail classifications - which design does it most appear like?

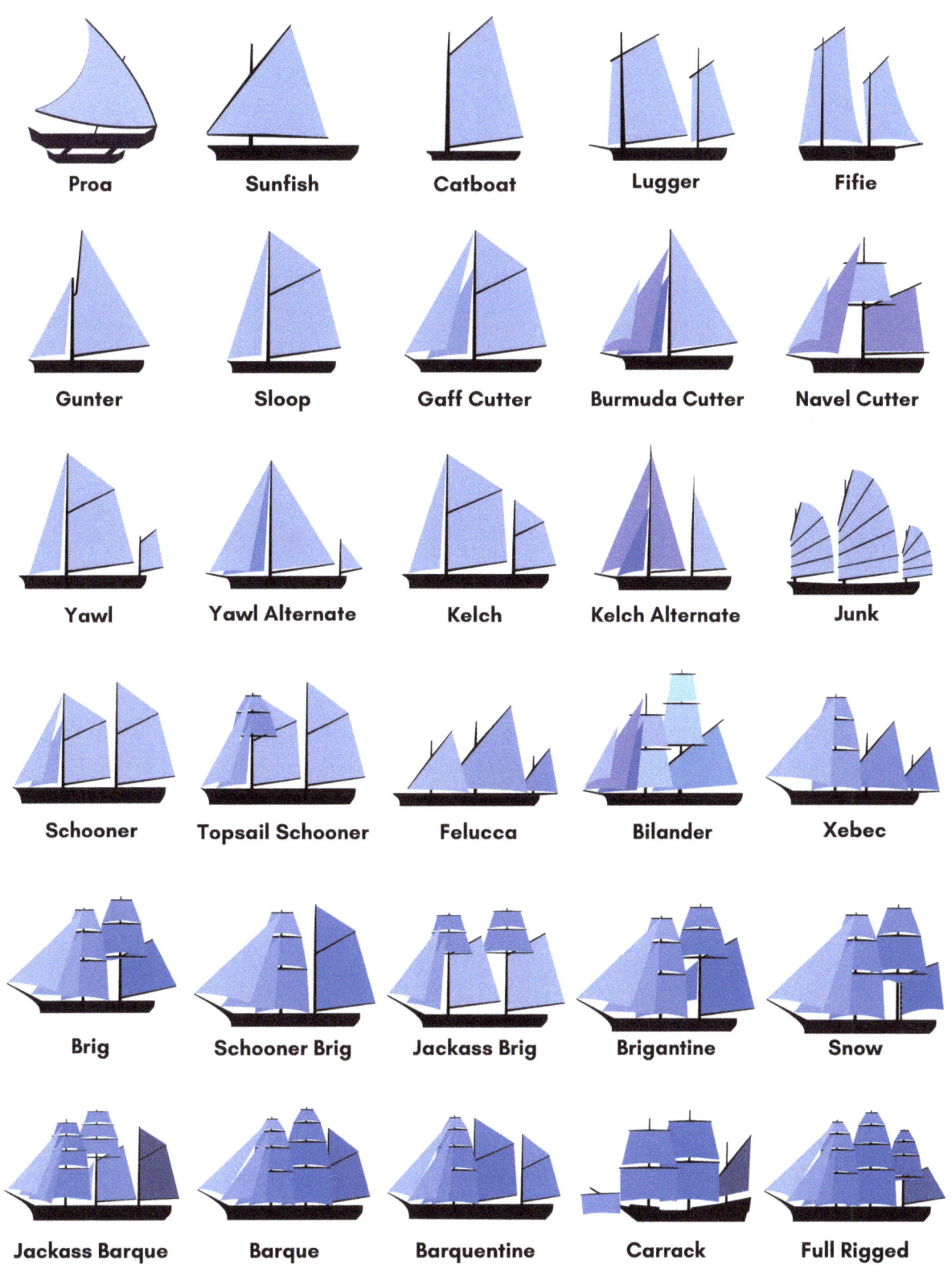

Antarctic Expeditions - Heroic Age

Belgica

Belgian Antarctic Expedition, 1897–1899

Captain: Adrien de Gerlache
Class: Barque
Length: 36 meters (118 feet)
Expedition: First ship to overwinter in the Antarctic
Current Location: Norwegian Sea, Norway

Southern Cross

British Antarctic Expedition, 1898–1900

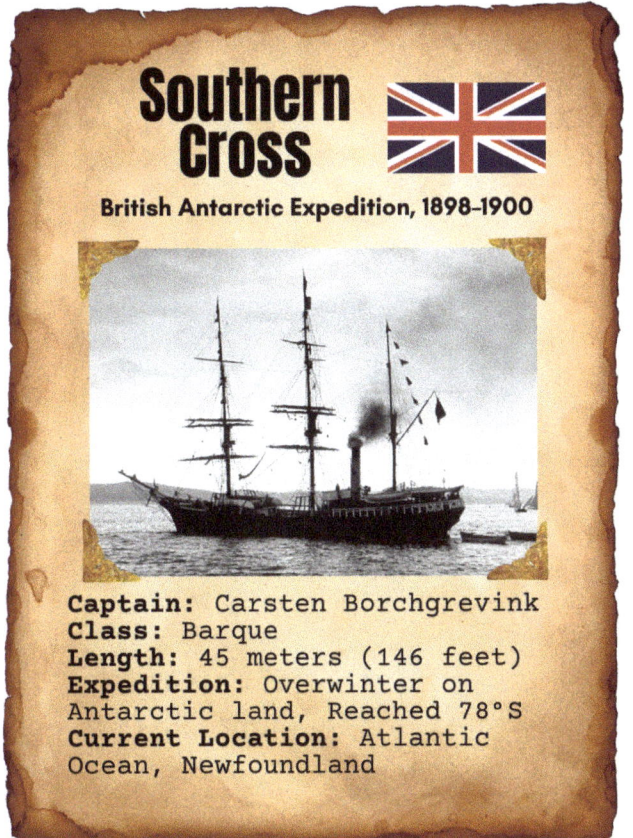

Captain: Carsten Borchgrevink
Class: Barque
Length: 45 meters (146 feet)
Expedition: Overwinter on Antarctic land, Reached 78°S
Current Location: Atlantic Ocean, Newfoundland

RRS Discovery

Discovery Expedition, 1901–1904

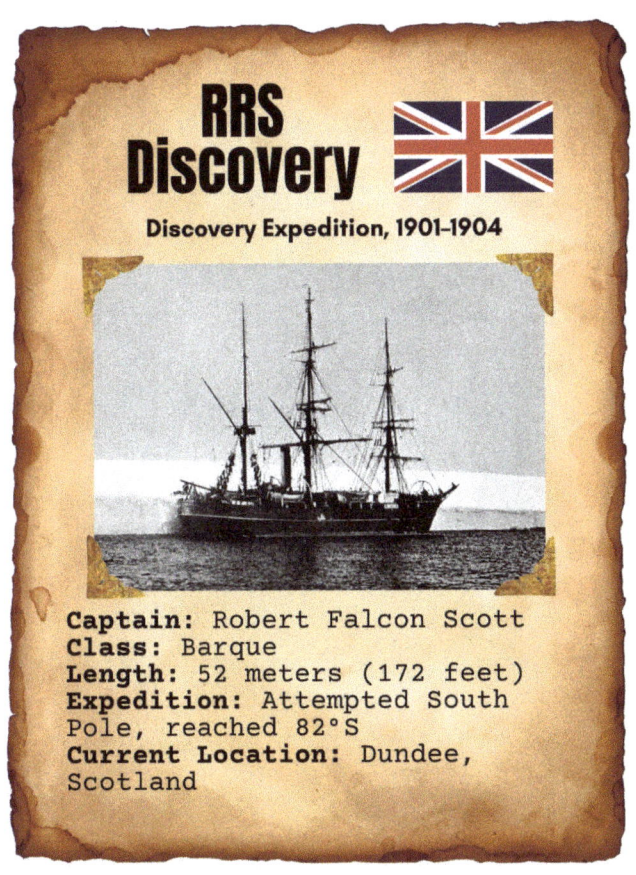

Captain: Robert Falcon Scott
Class: Barque
Length: 52 meters (172 feet)
Expedition: Attempted South Pole, reached 82°S
Current Location: Dundee, Scotland

Gauss

Gauss Expedition, 1901–1903

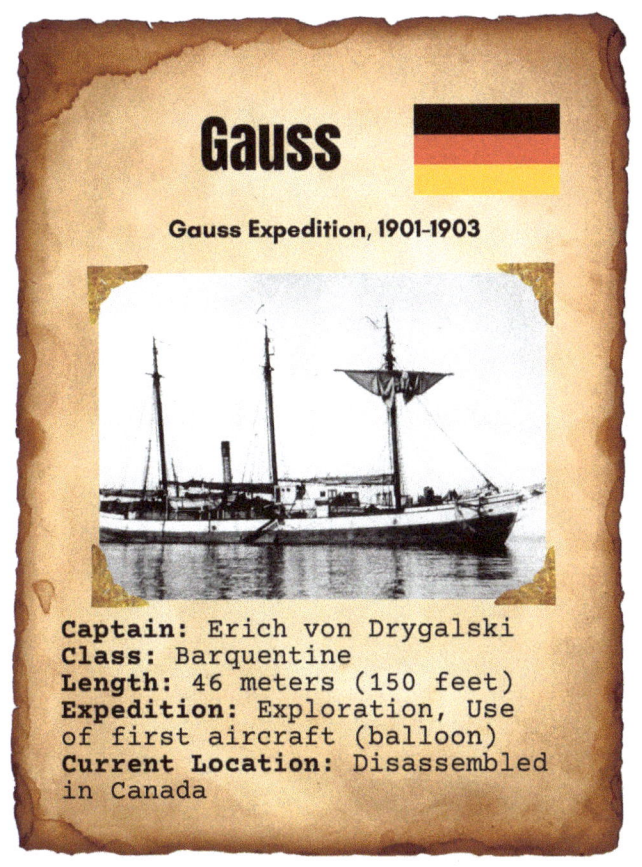

Captain: Erich von Drygalski
Class: Barquentine
Length: 46 meters (150 feet)
Expedition: Exploration, Use of first aircraft (balloon)
Current Location: Disassembled in Canada

Antarctic Expeditions - Heroic Age

Antarctic 🇸🇪
Swedish Antarctic Expedition, 1901-1903

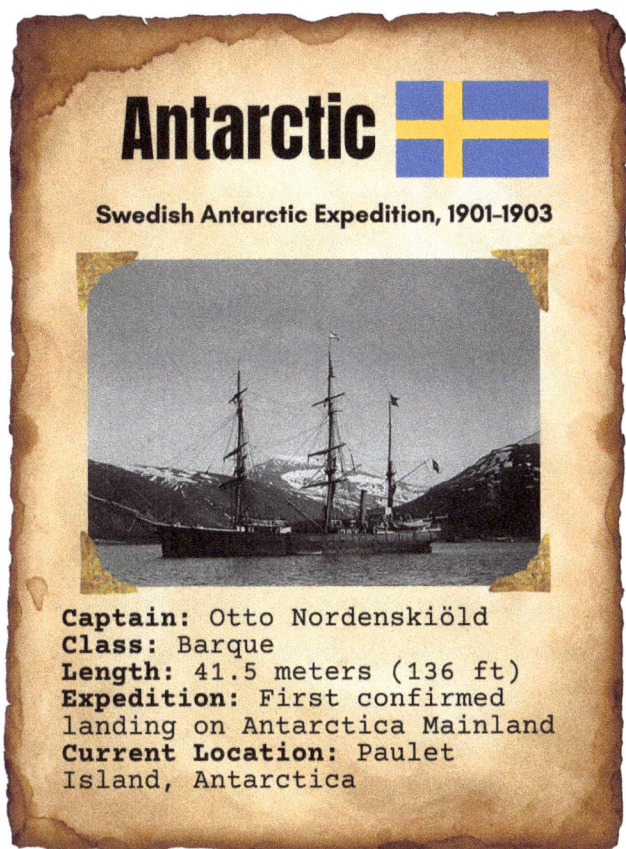

Captain: Otto Nordenskiöld
Class: Barque
Length: 41.5 meters (136 ft)
Expedition: First confirmed landing on Antarctica Mainland
Current Location: Paulet Island, Antarctica

Scotia 🇬🇧
Scottish National Antarctic Expedition, 1902-1904

Captain: William Speirs Bruce
Class: Barque
Length: 42.5 meters (139.5 feet)
Expedition: Established meteorological station
Current Location: Bristol Channel, Great Britain

Nimrod 🇳🇴
Nimrod Expedition, 1907-1909

Captain: Ernest Shackleton
Class: Schooner
Length: 41.5 meters (136 feet)
Expedition: Attempted South Pole, Reached 88°S, Climbed Mt. Erebus
Current Location: North Sea, Great Britain

Pourquoi-Pas 🇫🇷
French Antarctic Expedition, 1908-1910

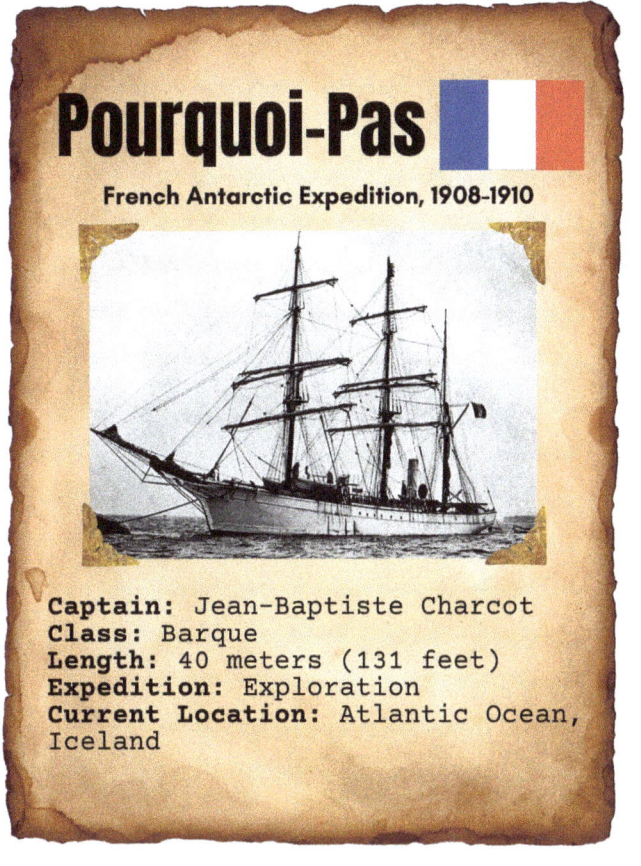

Captain: Jean-Baptiste Charcot
Class: Barque
Length: 40 meters (131 feet)
Expedition: Exploration
Current Location: Atlantic Ocean, Iceland

Antarctic Expeditions - Heroic Age

Kainan Maru 🇯🇵
Japanese Antarctic Expedition, 1910–1912

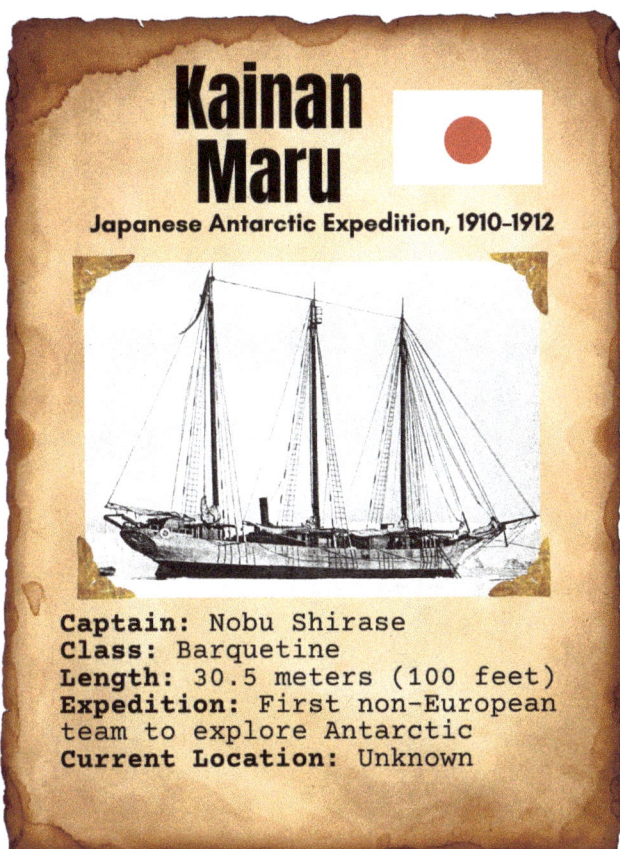

Captain: Nobu Shirase
Class: Barquetine
Length: 30.5 meters (100 feet)
Expedition: First non-European team to explore Antarctic
Current Location: Unknown

Fram 🇳🇴
Amundsen's South Pole Expedition, 1910–1912

Captain: Roald Amundsen
Class: Schooner
Length: 39 meters (127.5 feet)
Expedition: First to reach South Pole
Current Location: Oslo, Norway

Terra Nova 🇬🇧
Terra Nova Expedition, 1910–1913

Captain: Robert Falcon Scott
Class: Barque
Length: 57 meters (187 feet)
Expedition: Reached South Pole
Current Location: Labrador Sea, Greenland

Deutschland 🇩🇪
2nd German Antarctic Expedition, 1911–1913

Captain: Wilhelm Filchner
Class: Barque
Length: 48.5 meters (159 feet)
Expedition: Map geography of Antarctic continent
Current Location: Adriatic Sea

Antarctic Expeditions - Heroic Age

SY Aurora

Australasian Antarctic Expedition, 1911–1914

Captain: Douglas Mawson
Class: Barque
Length: 50 meters (165 ft)
Expedition: Exploration, first meteor found and radio use
Current Location: Tasman Sea, Australia

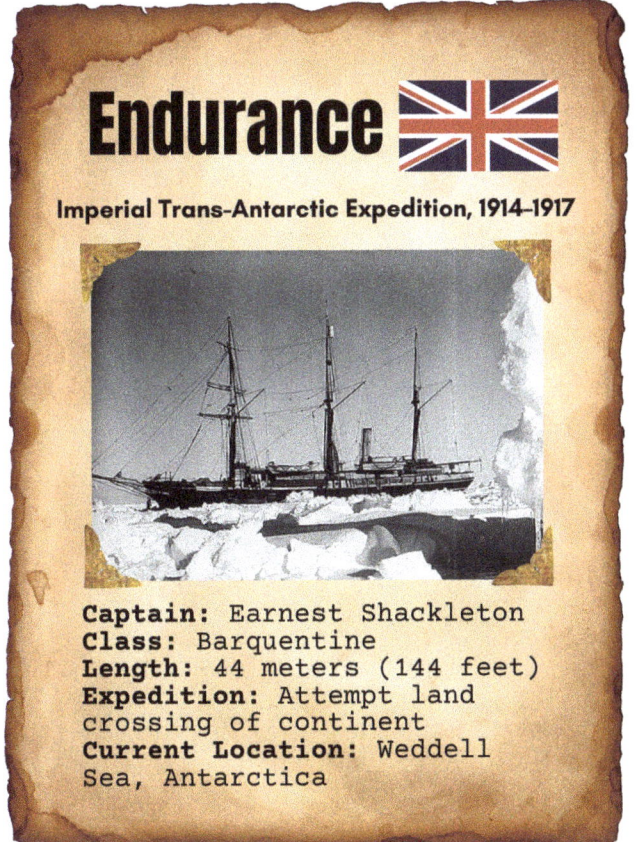

Endurance

Imperial Trans-Antarctic Expedition, 1914–1917

Captain: Earnest Shackleton
Class: Barquentine
Length: 44 meters (144 feet)
Expedition: Attempt land crossing of continent
Current Location: Weddell Sea, Antarctica

Snow Goggle Pattern

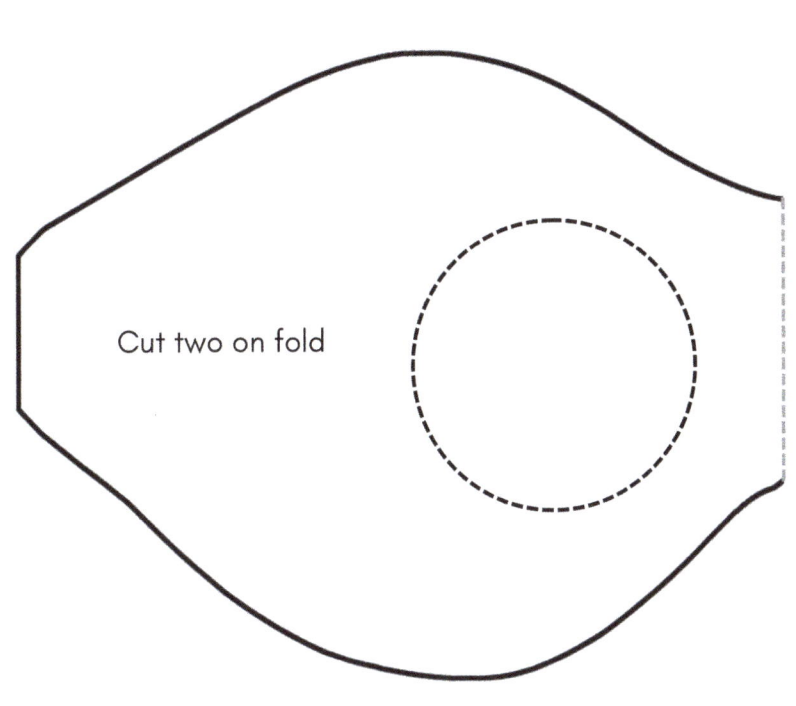

Cut two on fold

VINTAGE SNOW GOGGLES

Materials
- Goggle Pattern
- Scissors
- Felt
- Two Bottles w/Caps
- Plastic Sheet
- Elastic
- Fabric Glue

Instructions

Snow goggles were used to protect the eyes and to prevent snow blindness. This was a painful eye condition caused by exposure to sunlight reflected from snow and ice. Early goggles often struggled to provide enough protection without fogging up.

Snow goggles worn by Ernest Shackleton

Use included pattern to cut out two pieces of felt, along fold. Cut the tops of two clean/dry water bottles and glue them into the eye holes of the goggles with fabric glue. Make sure the tops of the bottle face outwards. Measure size of child's head and sew a piece of elastic onto each side of the glasses. Glue second piece of felt over top of the plastic "eyepieces" and over top of the elastic ends/sewing. Allow to dry completely. Use colored plastic to glue small piece of plastic over end of plastic top and trim edges. Modern goggles are often tinted as darker colors allow less light to pass through the lens and are best for excessive sunlight and glare.

Discuss: Compare craft to modern snow goggles. How do they differ? How are they the same? How do modern snow goggles avoid fogging?

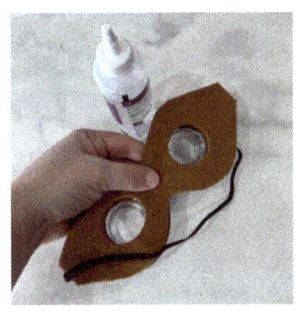
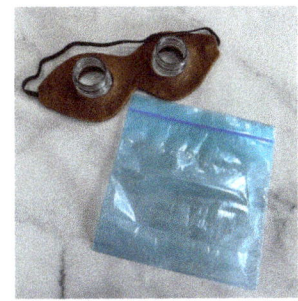

Antarctic Explorers

Cut out included explorers illustrations and stands. Cut small indentations into stand bottom as indicated by dashed lines. Cut out stand positioning strips and fold along center, as indicated. Cut indentation on strips and insert into stand bases. Adjust for best fit.

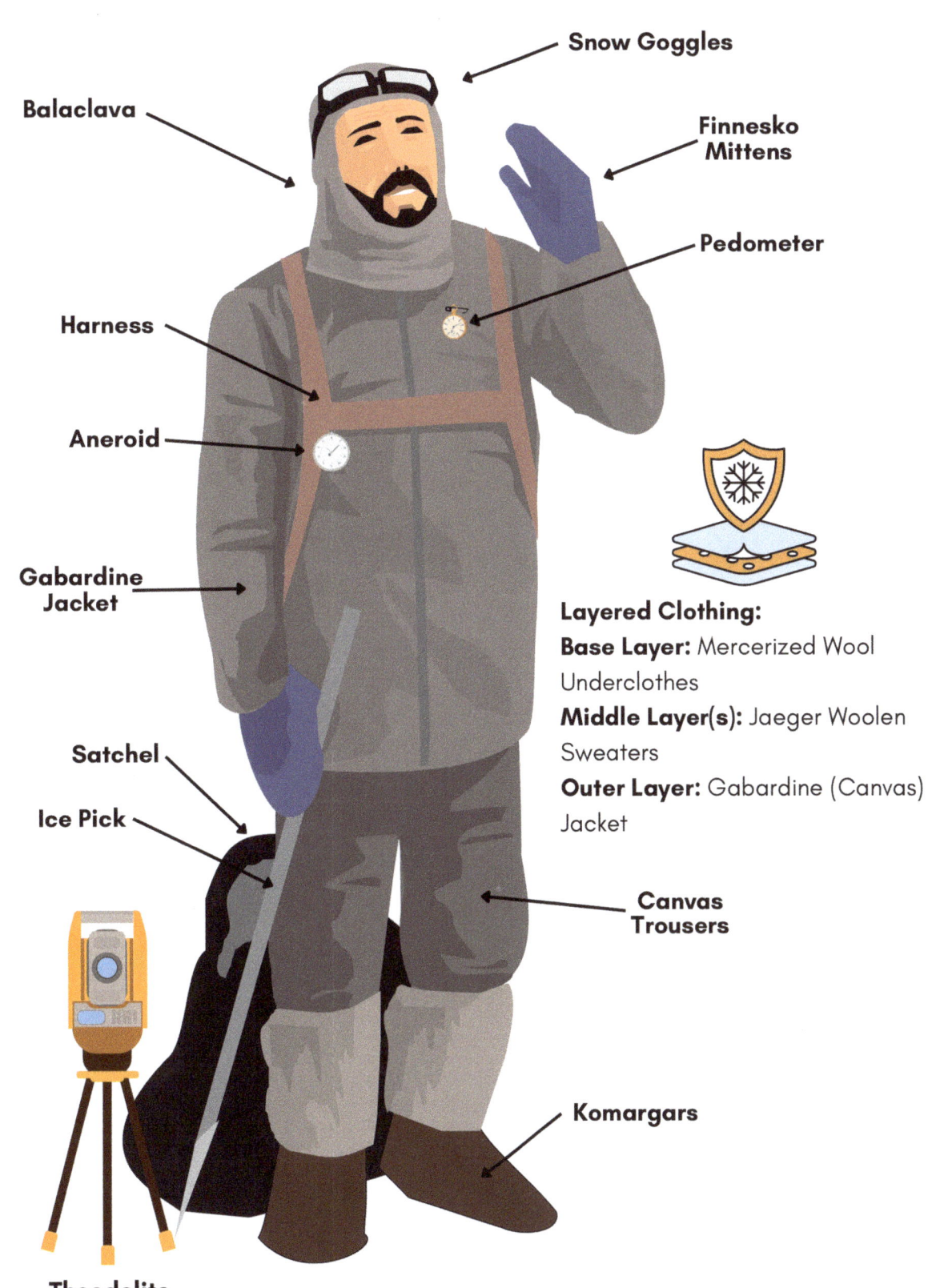

THE POLAR RACE

Even though Scott's expedition ended tragically, The *Terra Nova* returned to England with thousands of plants, animals, and fossils specimens, supporting the idea that Antarctica was once warm enough to grow trees and was connected to other landmasses. This expedition also provided baseline data for current research of climate change.

British explorer Robert Falcon Scott and Norwegian explorer Roald Amundsen were determined to be the first to reach the South Pole. Both had been to Antarctica before, and felt they had what it took to achieve this challenging feat.

9

2

In the early 20th century, nobody had ever been to the South Pole. However, many explorers wanted to earn a place in history by braving the freezing Antarctic.

1

In 1956, a permanent base was constructed at the South Pole, the *Amundsen-Scott South Pole Station*, which continues to be inhabited year-round. The legacy of these incredible explorers continues as researchers push the boundaries of what is known about this frozen continent and ultimately the world.

THE END.

10

Amundsen originally planned to conquer the North Pole, but in 1909 he learned explorers Cook and Peary had already reached it. Amundsen changed his plans to the South Pole, but he kept everything secret. In June of 1910, Amundsen set sail on the *Fram*, and finally told his crew they were going to Antarctica instead.

3

Amundsen and his crew returned without incident to their base camp in January of 1912, 99 days and about 1400 miles after their departure. Unfortunately, Scott and his team never returned. Their tent was found several months later. One of Scott's last entries in his diary stated, *"We took risks, we knew we took them; things have come out against us, and therefore we have no cause for complaint, but bow to the will of Providence, determined still to do our best to the last..."*

8

When Scott and his team finally reached the South Pole on January 17, 1912, he found a tent left by Amundsen. Inside was a letter from Amundsen, dated three weeks previous. Scott wrote in his diary, "*The worst has happened... All the day dreams must go... This is an awful place*".

Scott also set sail in June of 1910 on the *Terra Nova*. In October, as he was about to sail south from Australia, Scott received a telegram from Amundsen stating: "*Beg leave to inform you Fram proceeding Antarctic. Amundsen*".

The race was on.

Assembly Instructions

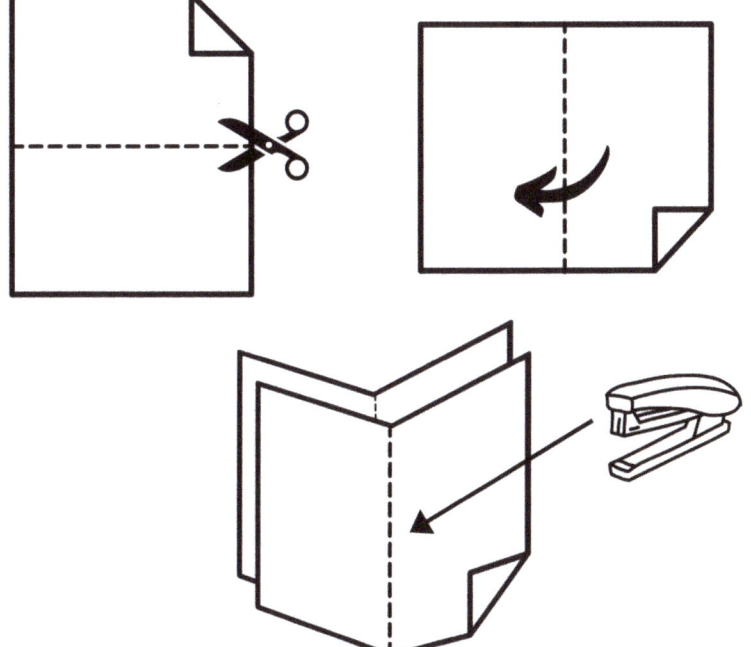

Cut paper in half on lines. Fold each page of book as indicated. Collate together so pages match up appropriately. Staple spine to hold together.

Amundsen reached the Ross Ice Shelf in January of 1911, and chose to land at the Bay of Whales. This gave his team a 60-mile advantage over Scott, who chose to land at McMurdo Sound. Upon their arrivals, Amundsen and Scott set up bases and prepared to endure the Antarctic winter.

Amundsen and his team set out for the South Pole in October of 1911. His team's ability to use skis and sled dogs provided them rapid and relatively trouble-free travel. On December 14, 1911, Amundsen raised the flag of Norway at the South Pole. He had reached his goal a full 33 days before Scott.

SNOW TRAVEL EXPERIMENT

Instructions

During the Heroic Age, many explorers struggled with effectively carrying equipment and supplies across Antarctica. Even modern transportation at the time was inadequate when faced with extreme cold, uneven landscape and sinking snow. In the race to the South Pole, Amundsen and Scott used different methods of transportation.

Materials
- Baking Soda
- White Conditioner
- Craft Stick
- Toy Car
- Rocks
- String
- Cooking Sheet

Faux Snow:
4 Cups Baking Soda
2/3 Cups Conditioner
Mix well to create a soft, crumbling snow.

Spread "snow" onto a cooking sheet, making sure the surface is uneven in places. Complete the following experiments:
- Tie string around toy car. Place rock on top of car and pull across snow.
- Tie string around paint stirrer. Place rock on top of wood and pull across snow.
- Tie string around rock, pull across snow.
- Hold rock in hand. Using pointer and index finger, walk across snow.

With each experiment consider the following:
- How did the weight of the rock affect the snow? *Consider weight to surface area distribution and observe the tracks on the snow.*
- What is the power source for this method (engine, animal, human)?
- What is required to maintain the power source (food, gas, temperature)?
- What areas of friction (resistance) were encountered when trying to move the load?
- How much additional force (effort) was required to transport the weight over uneven surfaces?

Record the results of each experiment on the included cards. **Discuss:** Which method of transportation is most effective?

SLED/SKIES

Circle the areas of the illustration touching the ground.

What is the power source? _____
What is required to maintain the power source? _____

What areas of friction were encountered? _____

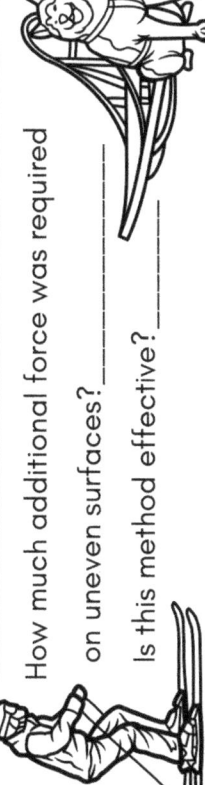

How much additional force was required on uneven surfaces? _____
Is this method effective? _____

CARRYING

Circle the areas of the illustration touching the ground.

What is the power source? _____
What is required to maintain the power source? _____

What areas of friction were encountered? _____

How much additional force was required on uneven surfaces? _____
Is this method effective? _____

WHEELS

Circle the areas of the illustration touching the ground.

What is the power source? _____
What is required to maintain the power source? _____

What areas of friction were encountered? _____

How much additional force was required on uneven surfaces? _____
Is this method effective? _____

PULLING

Circle the areas of the illustration touching the ground.

What is the power source? _____
What is required to maintain the power source? _____

What areas of friction were encountered? _____

How much additional force was required on uneven surfaces? _____
Is this method effective? _____

BANJO CRAFT

Instructions

Leonard Hussey was the meteorologist on Earnest Shackleton's ship, the "Endurance". As the crew abandoned ship, each sailor was allowed to bring only two pounds of personal possessions to face the brutal survivalist ordeal ahead. The 12-pound banjo, belonging to Hussy was an exception. Shackleton stated, *"It's vital mental medicine, and we shall need it."*

Materials
- Banjo Template
- Scissors
- Craft Glue
- Craft Sticks
- Paper Bowl
- String (Optional)

Cut out included banjo pieces. Glue the two pieces together along the neck, as indicated. Glue craft sticks along the neck to provide stability. Glue a paper bowl on back to create head. Allow to dry completely. *Optional:* Glue four strings down neck to enhance detail.

Listen to some banjo music. **Discuss:** What types of music do you enjoy? What instruments are used? Does music help you feel better when you are sad?

Leonard Hussey's Banjo

Checkers Game

Games were an important part of many expeditions to both the North and South Poles. Checkers is one type of game enjoyed by crew members of polar explorers, and some original boards are on display in museums around the world.

Checkers Game

Checkers Game Rules

Checkers is played by two players. The board is a 8 X 8 grid with alternating colors. Each player begins the game with 12 discs and places them on the 12 dark squares closest to their side. Each players alternate their turns, the first player is decided at random. Pieces can be moved diagonally and single pieces can only move forwards. A piece making a non-capturing move may move only one square. To capture an opponent's piece, the game piece must be able to "leap" over one of the opponent's pieces and lands in a straight diagonal line on the other side. This landing square must be empty. When a piece is captured, it is removed from the board. Only one piece may be captured in a single jump, but multiple jumps are allowed on a single turn. If a player is able to make the capture, then the jump must be made. When a piece reaches the furthest row, it is "crowned" with a discarded additional piece and becomes a king. Kings are limited to moving diagonally but can move both forward and backward. Kings may also combine jumps in several directions (forward and backward) on the same turn. A player wins the game when the opponent cannot make a move. This usually happens when all of the opponent's pieces have been captured, but it could also be because all of their pieces are blocked in.

Antarctica

A trip to:

What would you pack on your journey to Antarctica? What items would you need and why would you need them?

HOOSH

ingredients

- 1/2 Cup Dried Meat (or Plant-based) Jerky
- 1/2 Cup Crackers, Crushed
- 2 Tablespoons Butter
- 2 Cups Water

directions

Hoosh is a thick stew made from pemmican (a mix of dried meat and fat), thickener such as ground biscuits, and water. It was the common food of early twentieth century Antarctic expeditions.

- Chop jerky into small pieces, using a food processor or knife.
- Combine jerky, water and butter and bring to boil on stove. Reduce heat.
- Crush crackers. Add to mixture on stove. Add additional water if desired for consistency.
- Serve hot.

Hoosh

INGREDIENTS

CRACKERS

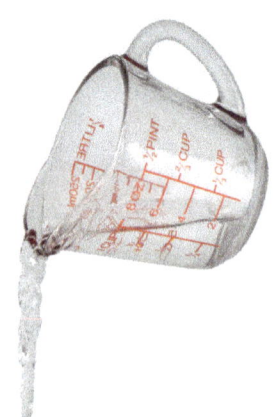

WATER

DRIED JERKY

BUTTER

PENGUIN POST OFFICE MODEL

Instructions

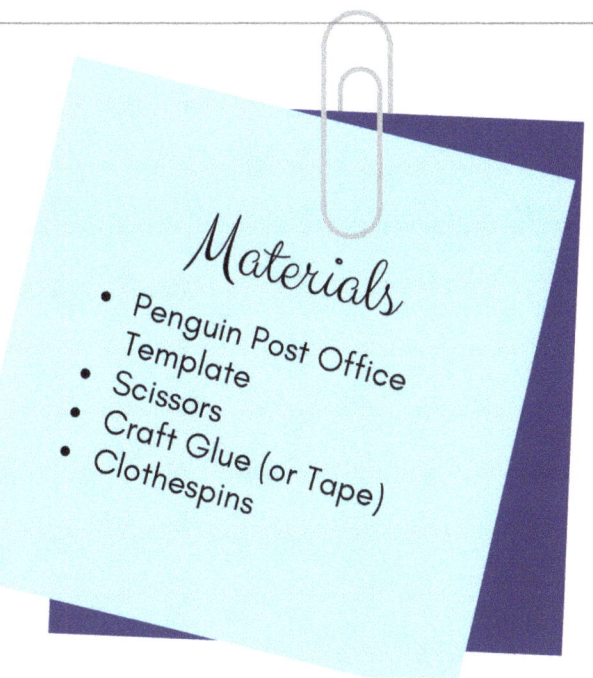

Materials
- Penguin Post Office Template
- Scissors
- Craft Glue (or Tape)
- Clothespins

The Penguin Post Office is a building in Port Lockroy, a historic British base. Located west of the Antarctic Peninsula, it is one of the most popular tourist destinations for cruise-ship passengers in Antarctica. The building now serves as a museum, post office and a location to count local penguins.

Cut out pieces. Fold sides and roof along indicated lines. Glue sides of building together, as indicated. It may be helpful to use clothespins to hold the pieces together while drying. Once base is drying, glue roof onto sides along tabs. Allow to dry completely.

Cut out the penguins. Cut slits into each penguin base. Cut out stand pieces. Fold in half and cut slits into the stands, as indicated. Insert stands over the slits in penguin base to create a triangular stand. Position penguins around the post office.

 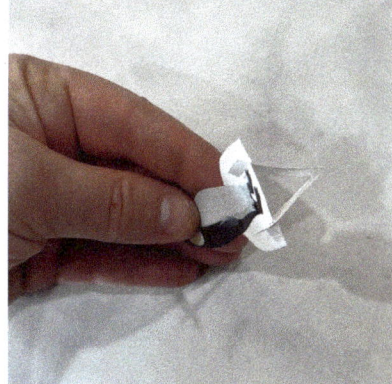 

Anatomy of a Postage Stamp

SERRATIONS

VALUE

DESIGN

ISSUING COUNTRY

INSCRIPTION

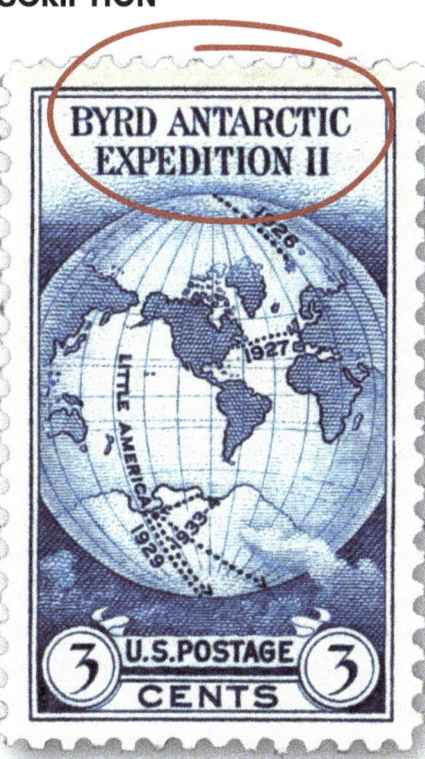

Design a Postage Stamp

Penguin Species Cards

Emperor
Aptenodytes forsteri

Height: 130 cm (50 inches)
Weight: 25-45 kg (55-100 pounds)

King
Aptenodytes patagonicus

Height: 94 cm (37 inches)
Weight: 13.5 to 16 kg (30 to 35 pounds)

Adélie
Pygoscelis adeliae

Height: 46 to 61 cm (18 to 24 inches)
Weight: 3.6 to 4.5 kg (8 to 10 pounds)

Chinstrap
Pygoscelis antarcticus

Height: 68–76 cm (27–30 inches)
Weight: 3.2–5.3 kg (7.1–11.7 pounds)

Penguin Species Cards

Gentoo
Pygoscelis papua

Height: 61 to 76 cm (24 to 30 inches)
Weight: 5.5 to 6.4 kg (12 to 14 pounds)

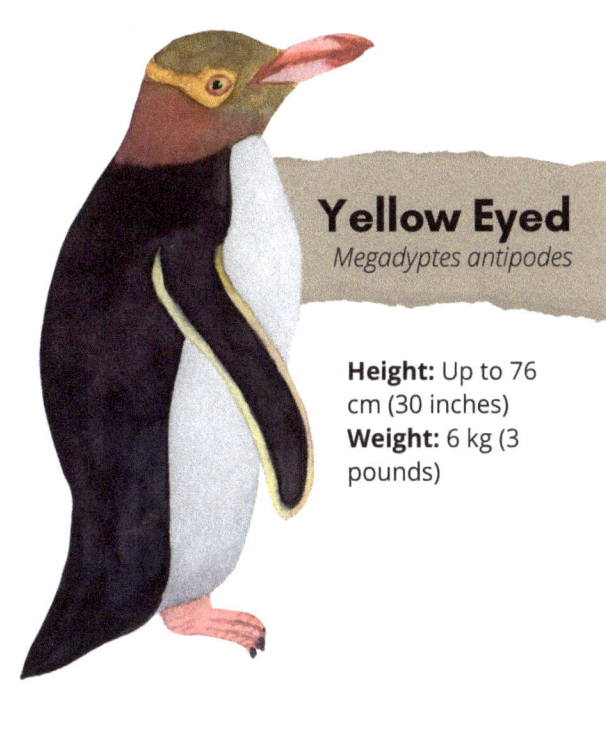

Yellow Eyed
Megadyptes antipodes

Height: Up to 76 cm (30 inches)
Weight: 6 kg (3 pounds)

Rockhopper
Eudyptes chrysocome

Height: 41 to 46 cm (16 to 18 inches)
Weight: 2.5 kg (5.6 pounds)

Fiordland
Eudyptes pachyrhynchus

Height: Up to 61 cm (24 inches)
Weight: 2.5 to 3 kg (6 to 7 pounds)

Penguin Species Cards

Erect Crested
Eudyptes sclateri

Height: up to 64 cm (25 inches)
Weight: 2.5 to 3.5 kg (6 to 8 pounds)

Macaroni
Eudyptes chrysolophus

Height: 51 to 61 cm (20 to 24 inches)
Weight: 4.5 kg (10 pounds)

Fairy
Eudyptula minor

Height: Up to 41 cm (16 inches)
Weight: Up to 1 kg (2 pounds)

Galapagos
Spheniscus mendiculus

Height: Up to 53 cm (21 inches)
Weight: Up to 2.5 kg (5.5 pounds)

Penguin Species Cards

Magellanic
Spheniscus magellanicus

Height: 61 to 71 cm (24 to 28 inches)
Weight: 5 kg (11 pounds)

Humboldt
Spheniscus humboldti

Height: 56 to 66 cm (22 to 26 inches)
Weight: 4 kg (9 pounds)

White Flippered
Eudyptula minor albosignata

Height: Up to 41 cm (16 inches)
Weight: Up to 1 kg (2 pounds)

African
Spheniscus demersus

Height: 60–70 cm (24–28 inches)
Weight: 2.2–3.5 kg (4.9–7.7 pounds)

Penguin Habitats

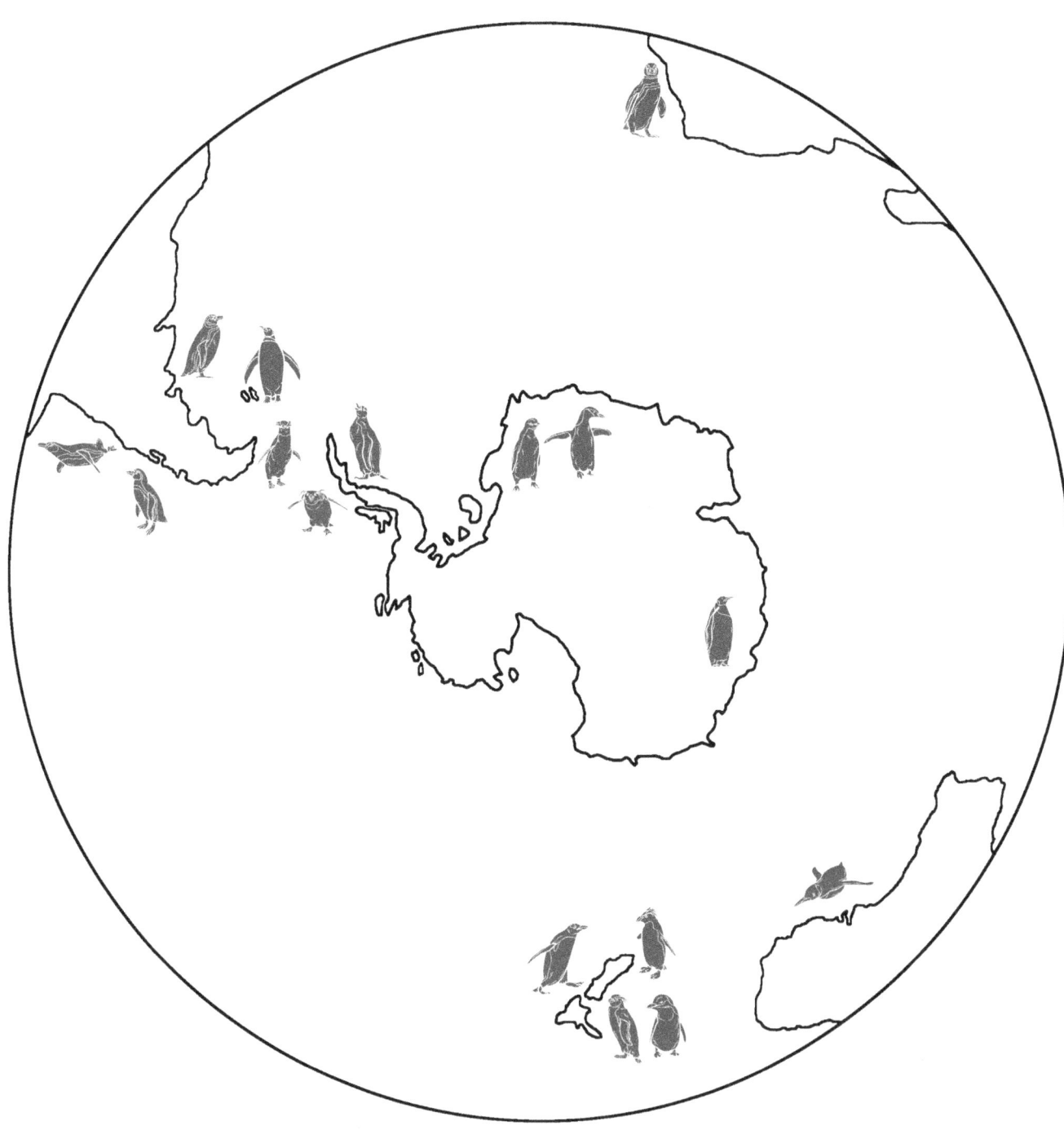

Units of Measurement - Penguins

Antarctica is home to eight different penguin species, living on the main continent and its nearby islands, and the sub-Antarctic archipelagos of South Georgia and the Falklands. Of these eight types of penguin, two live exclusively on Antarctica (Emperor and Adélie penguins), and the rest live in northern Antarctica and the sub-Antarctic islands.

Cut out the included rulers and penguin grid. Measure each penguin; compare the results. *Two rulers are provided to measure two penguins at the same time and compare.*

Life Cycle Spinner

Life Cycle of the *Penguin*

head	eye
bill	neck
tail	back	flipper	chest
flipper	webbed feet	claws	belly

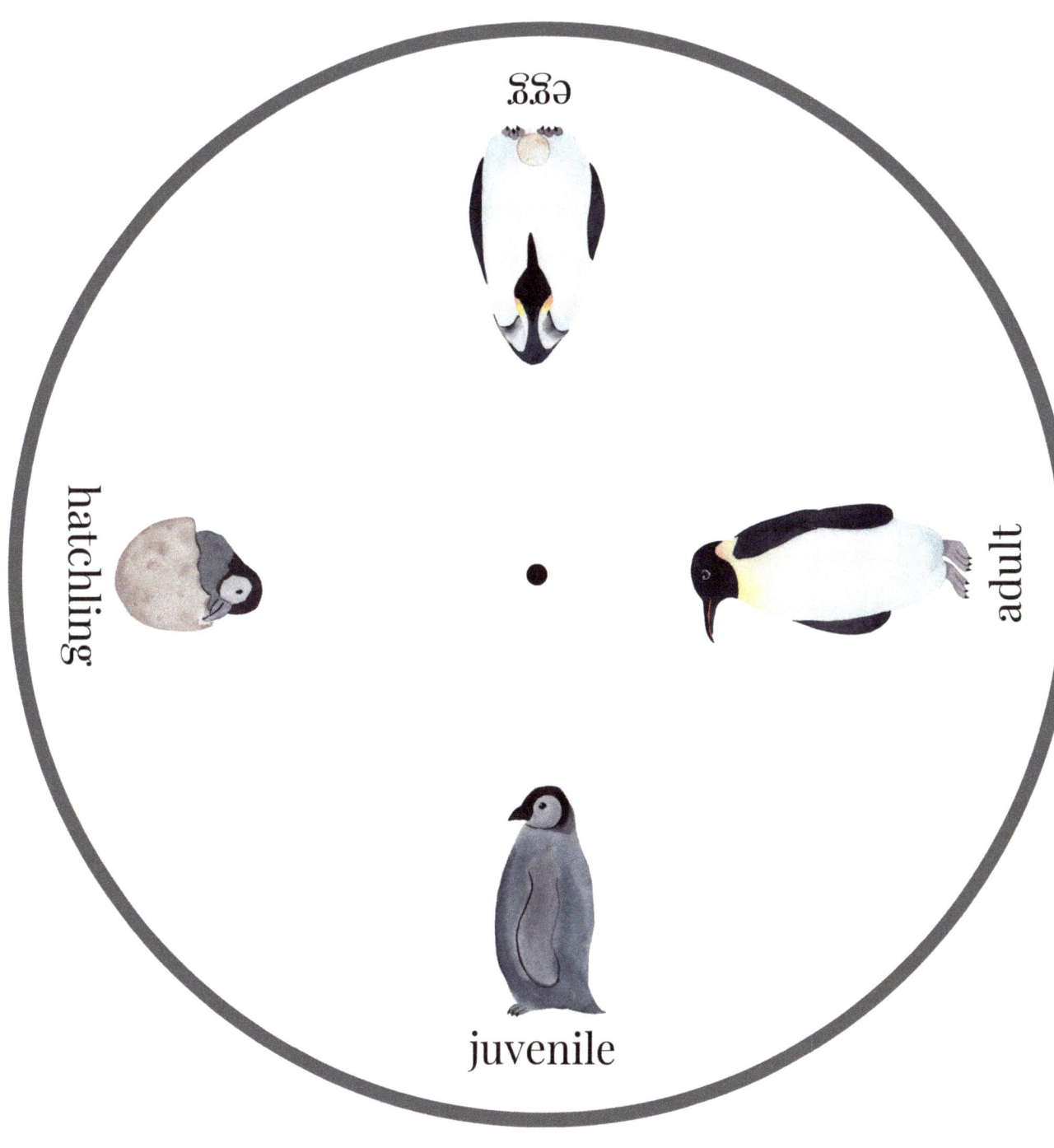

For use with felt puzzle

head	bill	eye	crest
neck	chest	belly	flipper
flipper	webbed feet	claws	

Anatomy of the Emperor Penguin

- head
- eye
- bill
- neck
- chest
- back
- flipper
- belly
- flipper
- tail
- webbed feet
- claws

Anatomy of the Emperor Penguin

Learning to Write

Penguin

Penguin

Penguin

Penguin

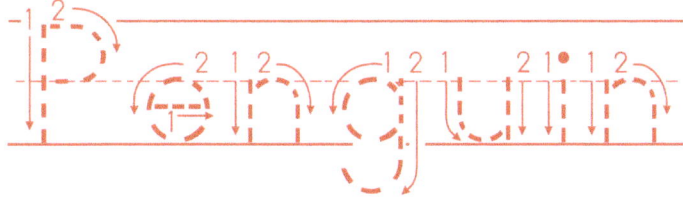

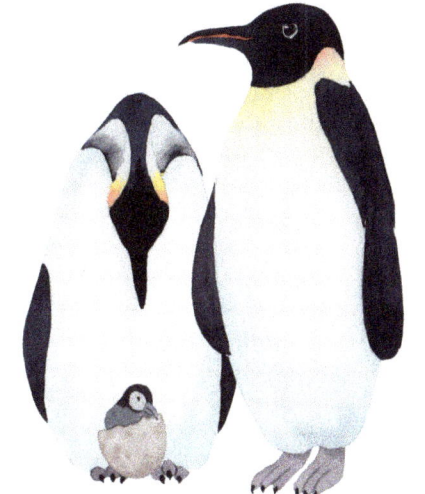

ROCKHOPPER PENGUIN FELT PUZZLE

Instructions

Antarctica is home to eight penguin species, with two (Emperor and Adélie) calling the continent their exclusive home. These animals have adapted well to the extreme cold of this unforgiving continent.

Cut out included puzzle pattern. Locate appropriate color of felt and trace pattern onto the felt with fine-tipped marker. Cut out each piece. Assemble pieces together and using the black outline as a base, stack the colors to create the detail, as indicated. Optional: glue smaller piece detail onto larger pieces to avoid them becoming lost with younger learners. Cut out included tags and match to appropriate features of the penguin.

Discuss: Compare and contrast the different penguin species - how do they differ? How are they the same? What features are not the same on all penguins?

Materials
- Felt
- Puzzle Patterns & Tags
- Marker
- Scissors
- Fabric Glue (Optional)

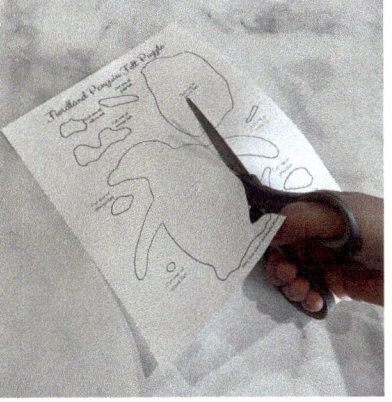
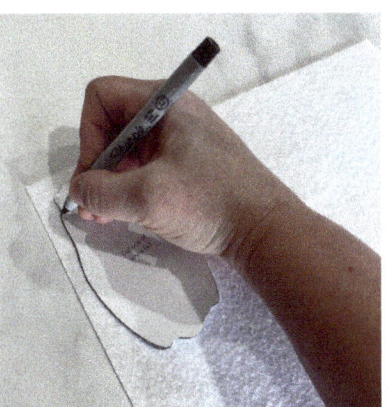
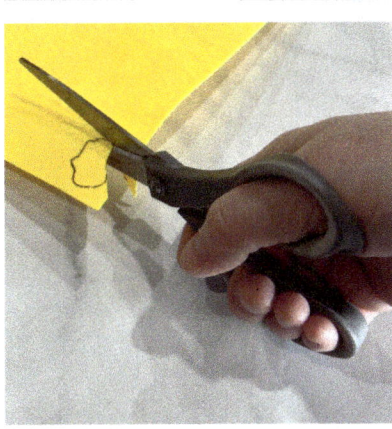

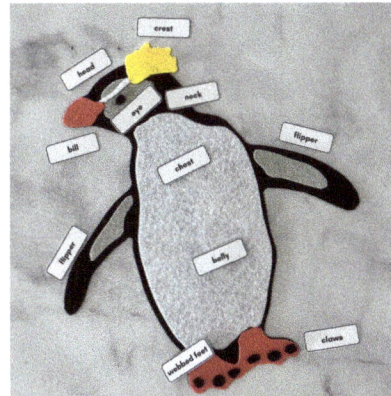

Rockhopper Penguin Felt Puzzle

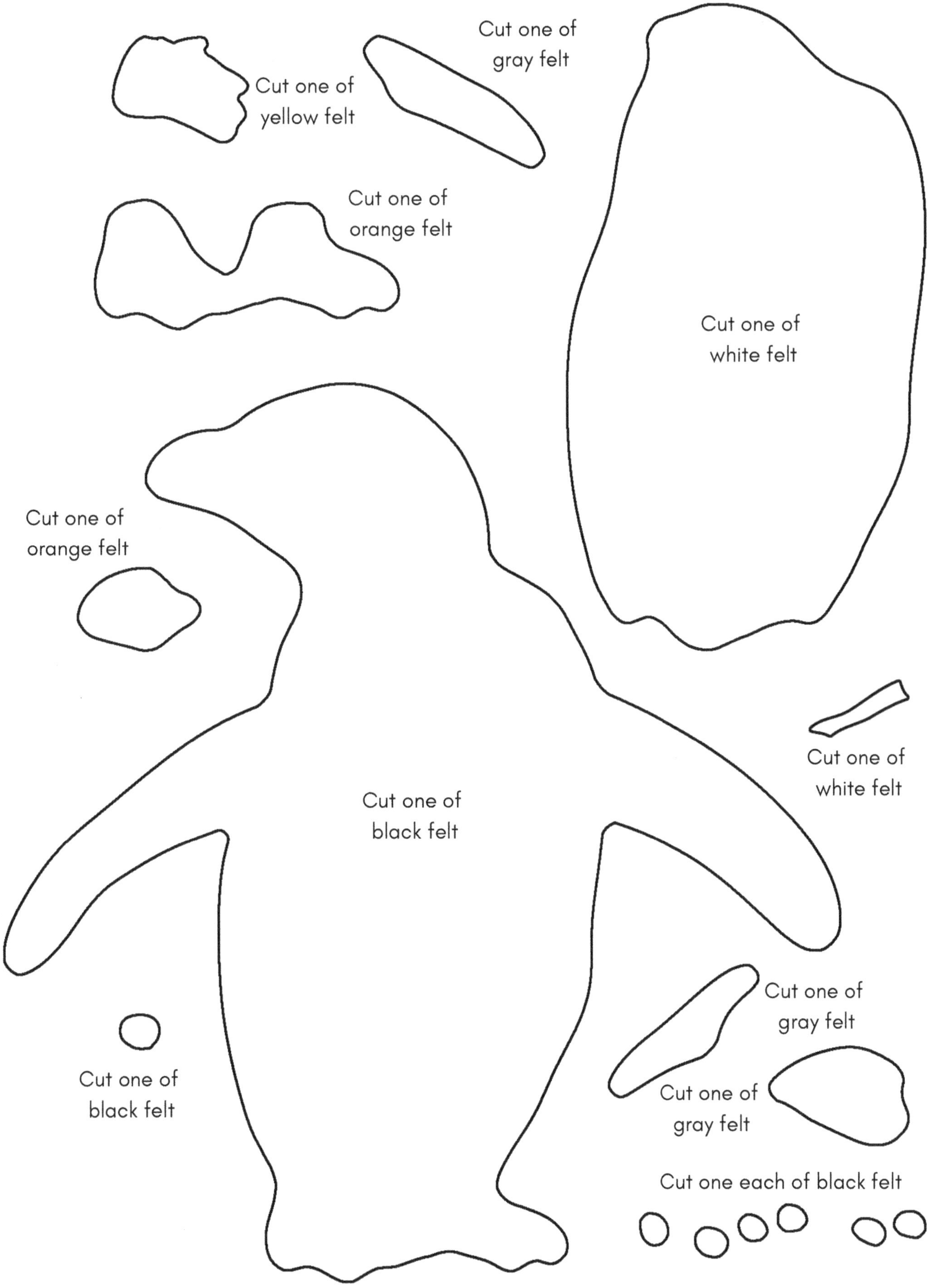

Cut one of yellow felt

Cut one of gray felt

Cut one of orange felt

Cut one of white felt

Cut one of orange felt

Cut one of black felt

Cut one of white felt

Cut one of gray felt

Cut one of gray felt

Cut one of black felt

Cut one each of black felt

Penguin Counting

Penguin Counting

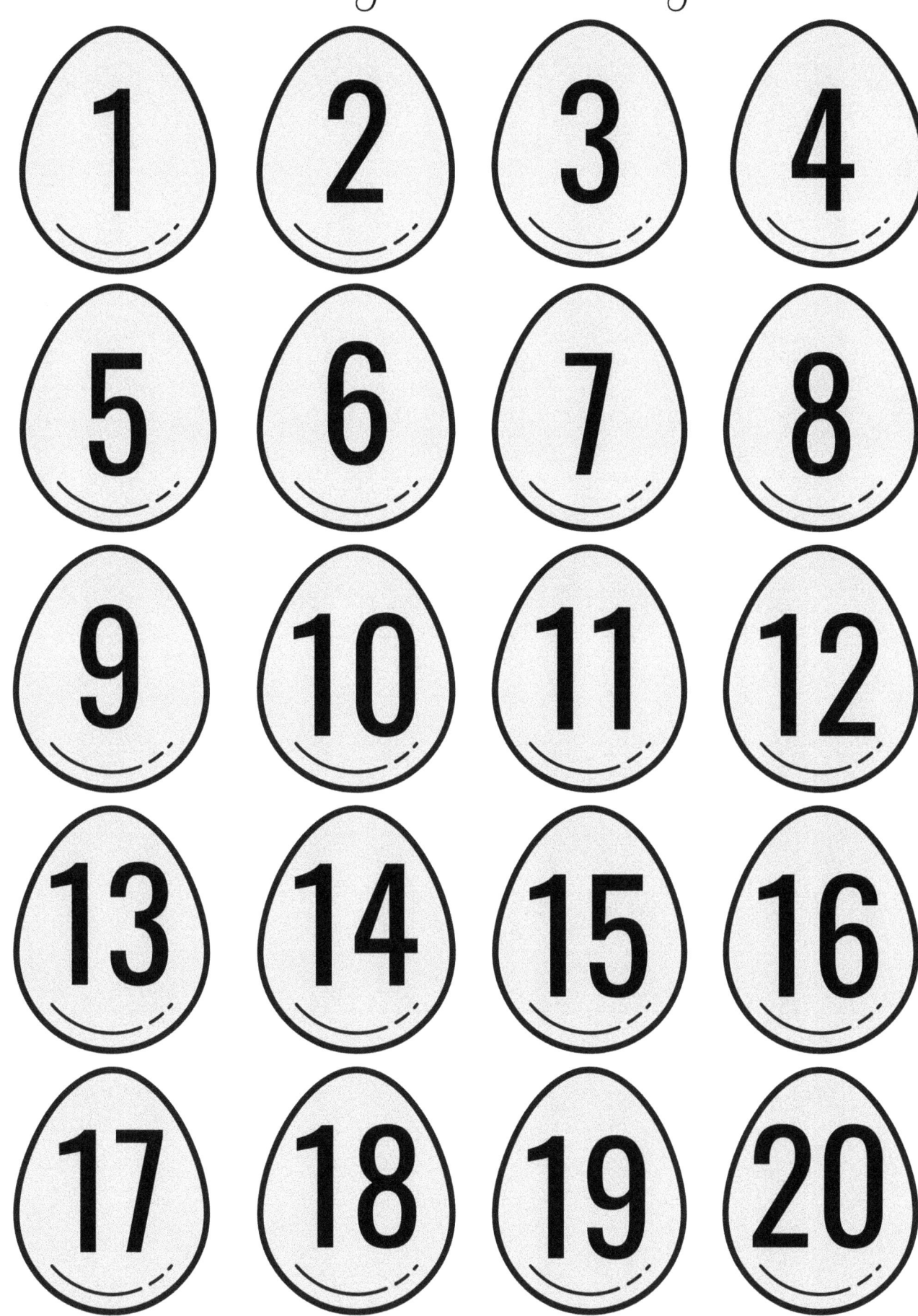

Penguin Counting

Use a **1.5 inch circle punch** to cut out the krill and use them to fill the penguin's belly with corresponding number of krill to the number on the egg.

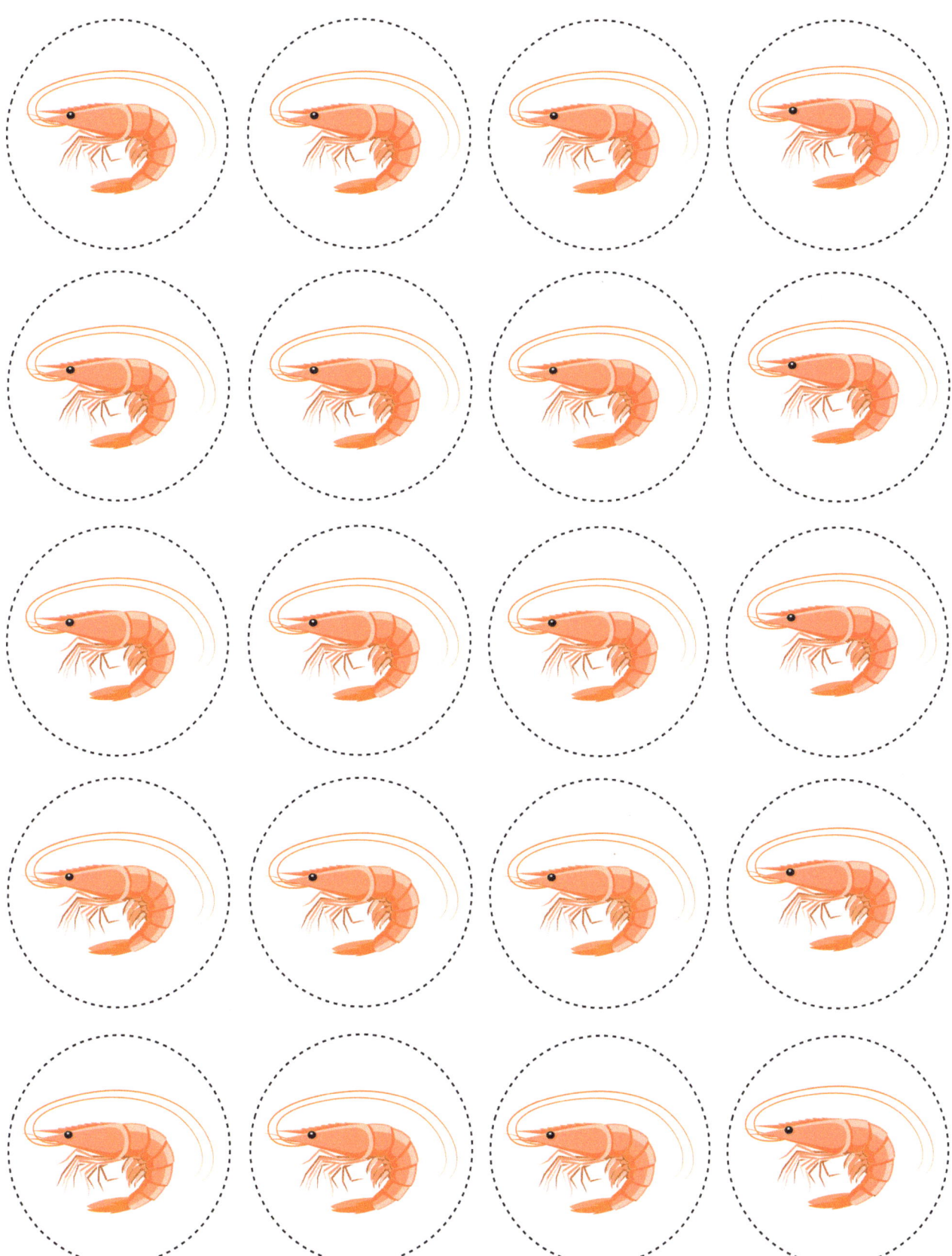

PENGUIN EGG WADDLE

Instructions

Emperor penguins are one of two species of penguins that call Antarctica their exclusive home. Emperor penguins breed annually during the Antarctic winter (June through August) and must contend with temperatures of -60° F and winds of up to 200 kph (124 mph). To keep the eggs warm, penguins wedge their eggs on the tops of their feet and covering them with their warm, overhanging bellies. They shuffle around in groups to preserve their body heat. The female goes to sea to feed while the male incubates the egg. Several weeks later she returns, usually just before the egg is ready to hatch, to relieve her mate so that he may also feed.

Blow up balloons. These are the penguin "eggs" - be careful not to "crack" them! Place between legs and on top of feet. Try to move while keeping the "egg" safe - don't let it touch the ground!

Materials
- Balloons

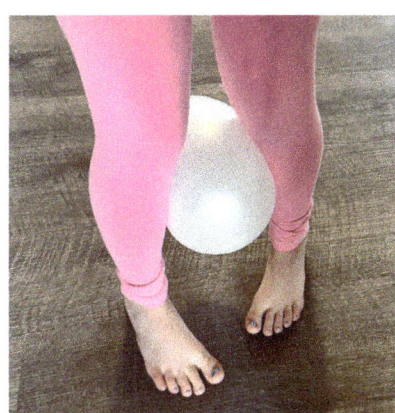

North vs. South Pole

North Pole

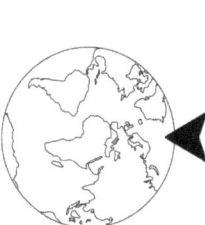

- Northernmost point of the Earth's axis.
- Floating ice sheets in Arctic Ocean with no land mass.
- Average winter temperature is -30° C.
- Highest elevation is sea level.
- The Arctic Circle includes parts of Canada, Greenland, Russia, Norway, Sweden and Finland.
- Polar bears are found here.
- Less ice than the South pole.
- Terrestrial mammals such as reindeer, musk ox, caribou, wolf, fox, etc. are found here.
- Native people live within the arctic circle.

(Intersection)

- Points of earth's axis.
- Receive six months of sunlight followed by six months of darkness.
- Sun never rises more than 23.5°
- Minimal solar radiation.
- Average temperature is below freezing.
- Longitude lines meet.

South Pole

- Southernmost point of the Earth's axis.
- Continent of Antarctica covered by ice sheets.
- Highest average elevation of any continent - averaging 2,500 meters (8,200 feet).
- Average winter temperature is -60° C.
- Only area on the Earth that does not belong to any country.
- Penguins are found here.
- 90% of the ice masses on Earth found here.
- Terrestrial mammals do not live here.
- No native people in this region.

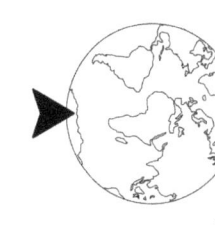

Arctic Desert

Climate
The average annual temperature is well below freezing, averaging as cold as −60°C. Winds can also be a significant factor, reaching hurricane levels in some areas.

Flora
Due to extremely cold temperatures, minimal sunlight and moisture, poor soil quality, and a short growing period, this biome is inhospitable to most species of flora. Still, some varieties of lichens, mosses, and algae still manage to thrive.

Fauna
Most animals living here have adapted to the harsh conditions, with layers of fat and fur protecting them from the elements. Fauna varies from geographical locations, but includes mammals, birds, fish, and invertebrates.

Water
Because minimal precipitation (rain or snow) occurs here, it is classified as a desert. Most precipitation becomes ice that covers the landscape. Around 90% of the world's surface fresh water is held in the ice sheets of Antarctica.

Arctic Desert Habitat Matching

Cut out circles of animals and match into appropriate habitat.

Antarctic Animal Finger Puppets

Types of Antarctica Fauna

Antarctic Hair Grass
Deschampsia antarctica

Antarctic Pearlwort
Colobanthus quitensis

Lichen
Caloplaca

Moss
Grimmia antarctici

SEAL PUPPET

Instructions

Seals and sea lions are one of the few groups of marine mammals that live in the Antarctic. Seals are divided into two groups - true (earless) seals and fur seals which have small flaps over their ears, which are related to sea-lions. The Antarctic fur seals is one of the most abundant species of fur seal, and lives in the waters around Antarctica.

Color included seal template with crayons or markers. Cut out each piece. Glue mouth into side of folded bag crevice. Glue head on top and overlap jaw. Fold tabs on side of flippers and glue at an angle on the front, allowing them to "flap" if desired. Place hand in bag and four fingers into bottom portion of the bag and thumb wrapping around the folded portion. Open and shut hand to allow seal to "bark".

Discuss: Listen to a seal barking. Attempt to replicate this sound. Have somebody compare - how close did you do?

Seal Puppet

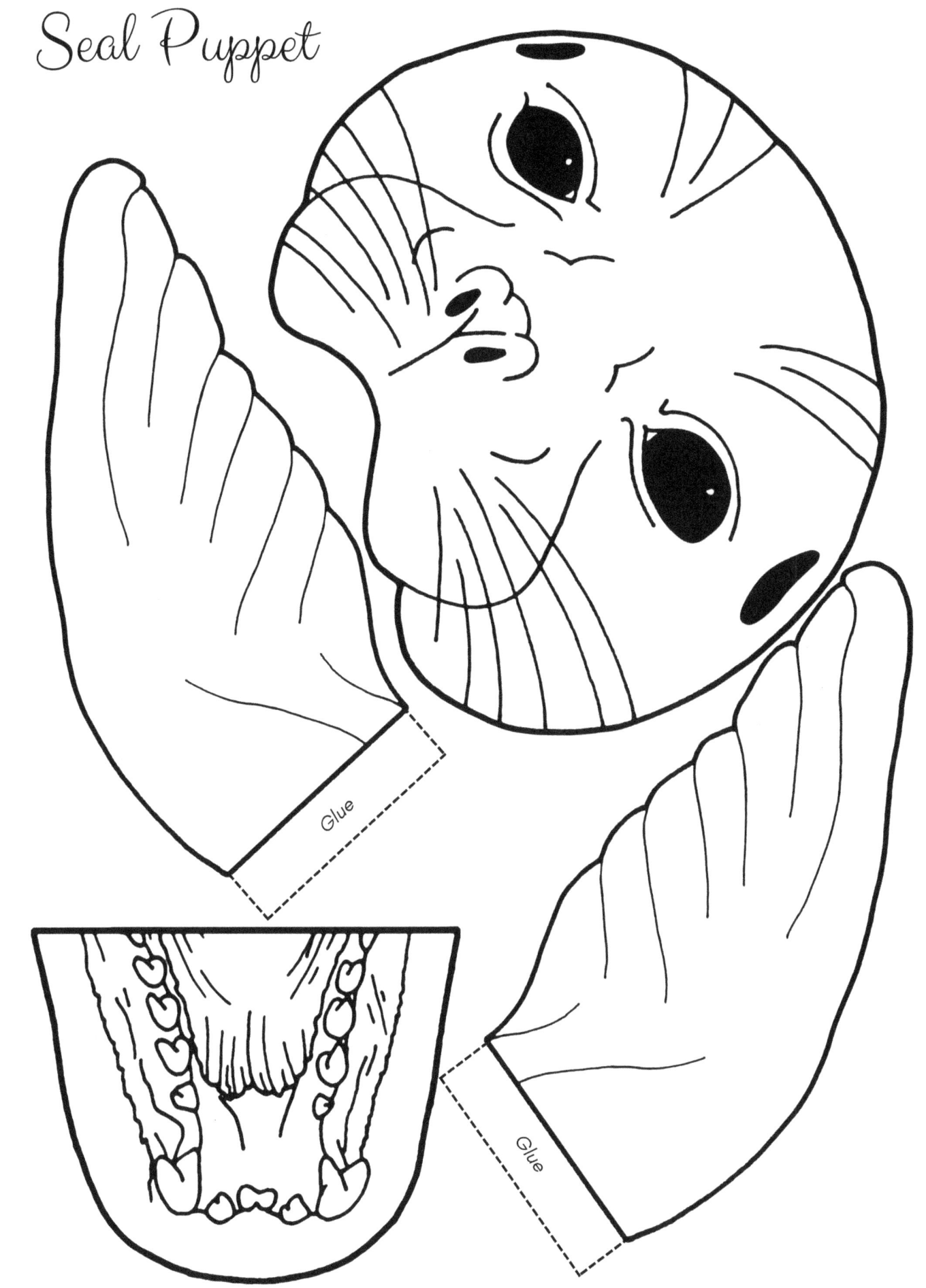

BLUBBER EXPERIMENT

Instructions

Blubber is an important adaptation for many marine mammals, especially those that live in icy waters. The thick layer of fat provides insulation from extreme temperatures, while also providing energy that can be used when food is unavailable.

Materials
- Mixing Bowl
- Ice
- Water
- Shortening
- Plastic Bags

Fill mixing bowl with ice and water. Coat the inside of plastic bag with shortening. Insert a second plastic bag to create pocket with a layer of shortening between both bags.

Have child place hands in ice water. Have them describe how the temperature feels. Place hand in shortening-lined bag. Place hand back in water; how does the temperature feel now? **Discuss:** What type of animals have blubber? Where do they live? Is this habitat warm or cold? What is the average temperature of the water they live in? What is the average temperature of the land?

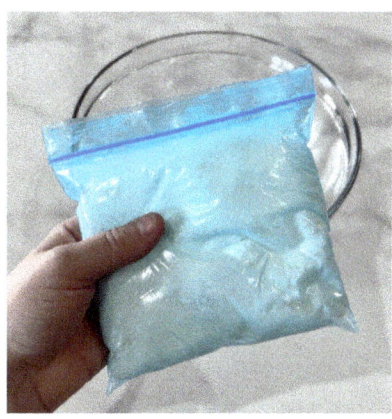
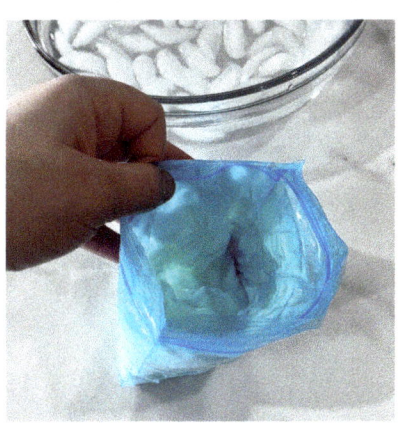

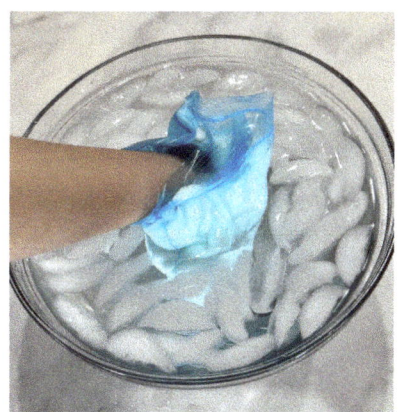

GLACIER MELT EXPERIMENT

Instructions

Approximately 10% of land area on Earth is covered with glacial ice. Almost 90% is in Antarctica, while the remaining 10% is in Greenland. Glacier melting is a concern because it raises sea levels, affects currents, pH, weather patterns and animal population. Temperature is not the only variable that affects how fast a glacier melts. Size and additives can also affect how fast the unfreezing process takes.

Materials
- Four Containers
- Casserole Pan
- Rocks
- Sand
- Water
- Mallet

Locate four containers of similar size. Fill one with rocks, one with sand and leave the remaining two to fill with water. Place in freezer and allow to freeze solid. Remove each from containers. Crush one of the plain water ice chunks to create smaller cubes of ice (do this over a non-breakable surface) and place all four examples in a pan. Observe the changes without disturbing further. **Discuss:** Which melts fastest? Consider the size and additives (rocks or sand) on each example.

Types of Glaciers

ICE SHEET

An ice sheet is a mass of glacial ice that exceeds 50,000 square kilometers (19,000 square miles). Ice sheets contain over 90% of the freshwater on Earth, and are sometimes known as continental glaciers. Ice sheets that extend beyond the coast and over the ocean are ice shelves. Ice sheets are only found in Antarctica and Greenland.

Ross Ice Shelf, Antarctica

ICE FIELD/CAP

Ice fields and caps are masses of glacial ice less than 50,000 square kilometers (19,000 square miles). Ice fields are constrained by topographical features, meaning their topography is determined by the shape of the surrounding landforms. By contrast, ice caps are not constrained by topographical features. Both are found in colder climates and higher altitudes.

Vatnajökull, Iceland

Types of Glaciers

ALPINE GLACIER

An alpine glacier is surrounded by mountain terrain. Alpine glaciers form over a cirque or high rock basin, and the uppermost layer becomes frozen solid, but the ice beneath behaves like a flexible substance, slowly moving their bodies of snow by gravity.

Crowfoot Glacier, Canada

VALLEY GLACIER

Valley glaciers are flowing ice confined within valleys. The downward erosive action of the ice carves the valley further. Glacial ice flowing down hill will follow existing valleys or areas of least resistance, eroding and enlarging them as it moves. If a valley glacier spills out of the mountains, the ice often spreads to form a lobe, called a piedmont glacier.

Aletsch Glacier, Switzerland

Types of Glaciers

TIDEWATER GLACIER

Glaciers that flow out of the mountains and down to the sea are called tidewater glacier. Freshwater glaciers are created when the glacier meets a freshwater source. Melting tidewater glaciers change the chemical properties of the ocean, decreasing the pH. This acidification can have adverse effects on marine wildlife habitat and populations.

Columbia Glacier, United States

ROCK GLACIER

Rock glaciers are distinct landforms, consisting of masses of rock, ice, snow, mud, and water that moves slowly down an area of high elevation by gravity. Rock glaciers are normally found at high elevations, and may extend outward and downward.

Khumbu Glacier, Tibet

Snowflake Shape Matching

Prism	Column	Sheath	Capped Plate	Triangular
Hexagon Plate	Hollow Column	Cup	Column Plate	12-Star
Stellar Plate	Bullet Rosettes	Capped Column	Split Plate	Radiating Plate
Sectored Plate	Bullet	Multiple Capped Column	Stacked	Radiating Dendrite
Star	Needle	Capped Bullet	Twin Column	Irregular
Stellar Dendrite	Needle Cluster	Double Plate	Arrowhead	Rimed
Fernlike Stellar Dendrite	Crossed Needle	Hollow Plate	Crossed Plate	Graupel

Snowflake Shape Matching

Prism	Column	Sheath	Capped Plate	Triangular
Hexagon Plate	Hollow Column	Cup	Column Plate	12-Star
Stellar Plate	Bullet Rosettes	Capped Column	Split Plate	Radiating Plate
Sectored Plate	Bullet	Multiple Capped Column	Stacked	Radiating Dendrite
Star	Needle	Capped Bullet	Twin Column	Irregular
Stellar Dendrite	Needle Cluster	Double Plate	Arrowhead	Rimed
Fernlike Stellar Dendrite	Crossed Needle	Hollow Plate	Crossed Plate	Graupel

PAPER SNOWFLAKES

Materials
- Snowflake Pattern
- Paper
- Scissors

Instructions

Water molecules in the solid state form weak bonds (called hydrogen bonds) to one another. During the freezing process, this results in the symmetrical, hexagonal shape of the snowflake. Although there are many classifications of snow flakes, the majority can be categorized into a few basic designs.

Cut out included snowflake patterns.
Use the larger pattern for larger pieces of paper (craft roll) and the smaller pattern for smaller pieces of paper (printer paper). Fold paper in half. Identify the center of the half and fold across from center about 1/3 across. Repeat with other side to create a three-layer triangular fold, as indicated. Place pattern over folded paper and cut out along dashed lines. Repeat with different size paper to create examples of different sizes.

Have child trace included labels. Label each snowflake with appropriate label.

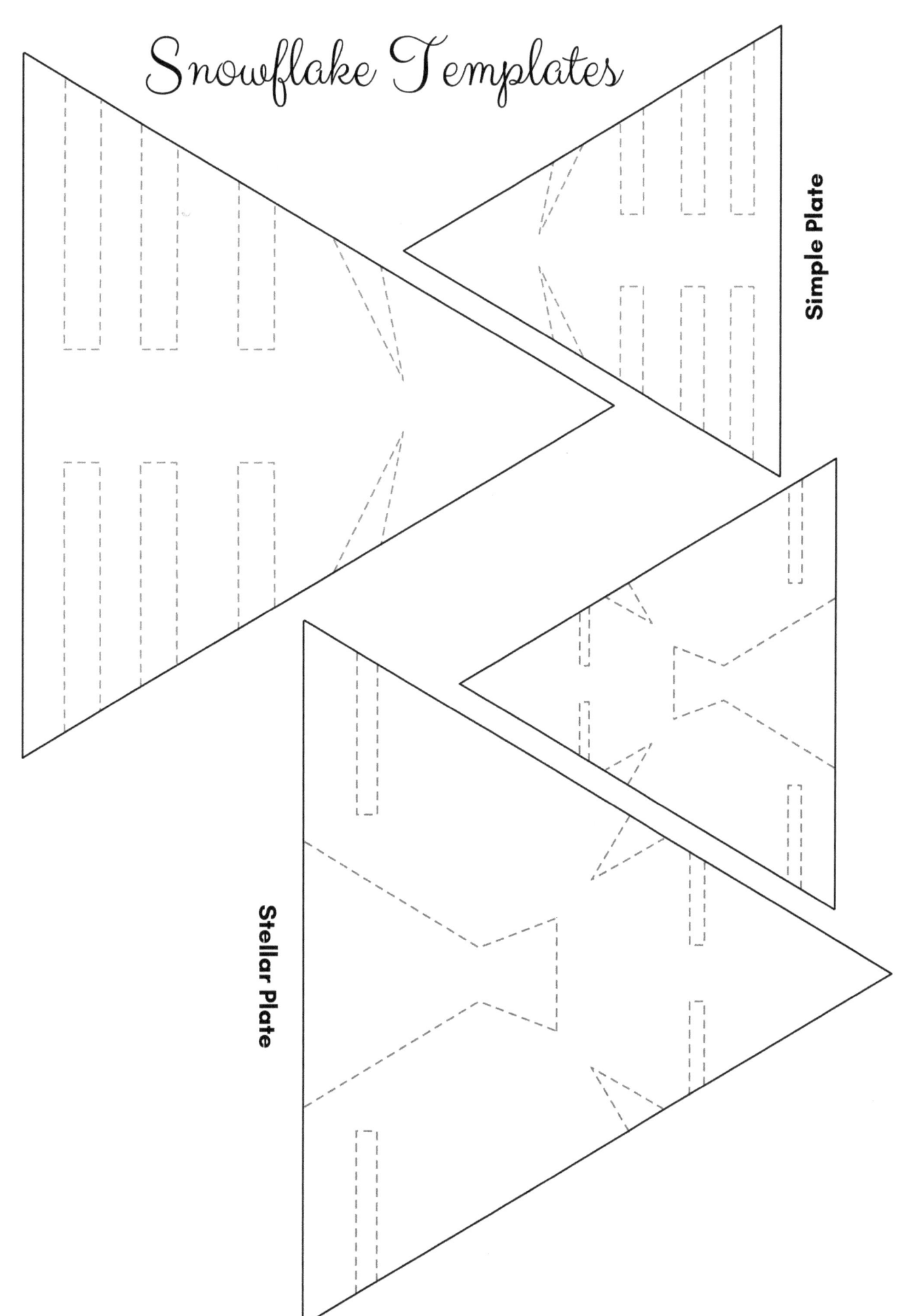

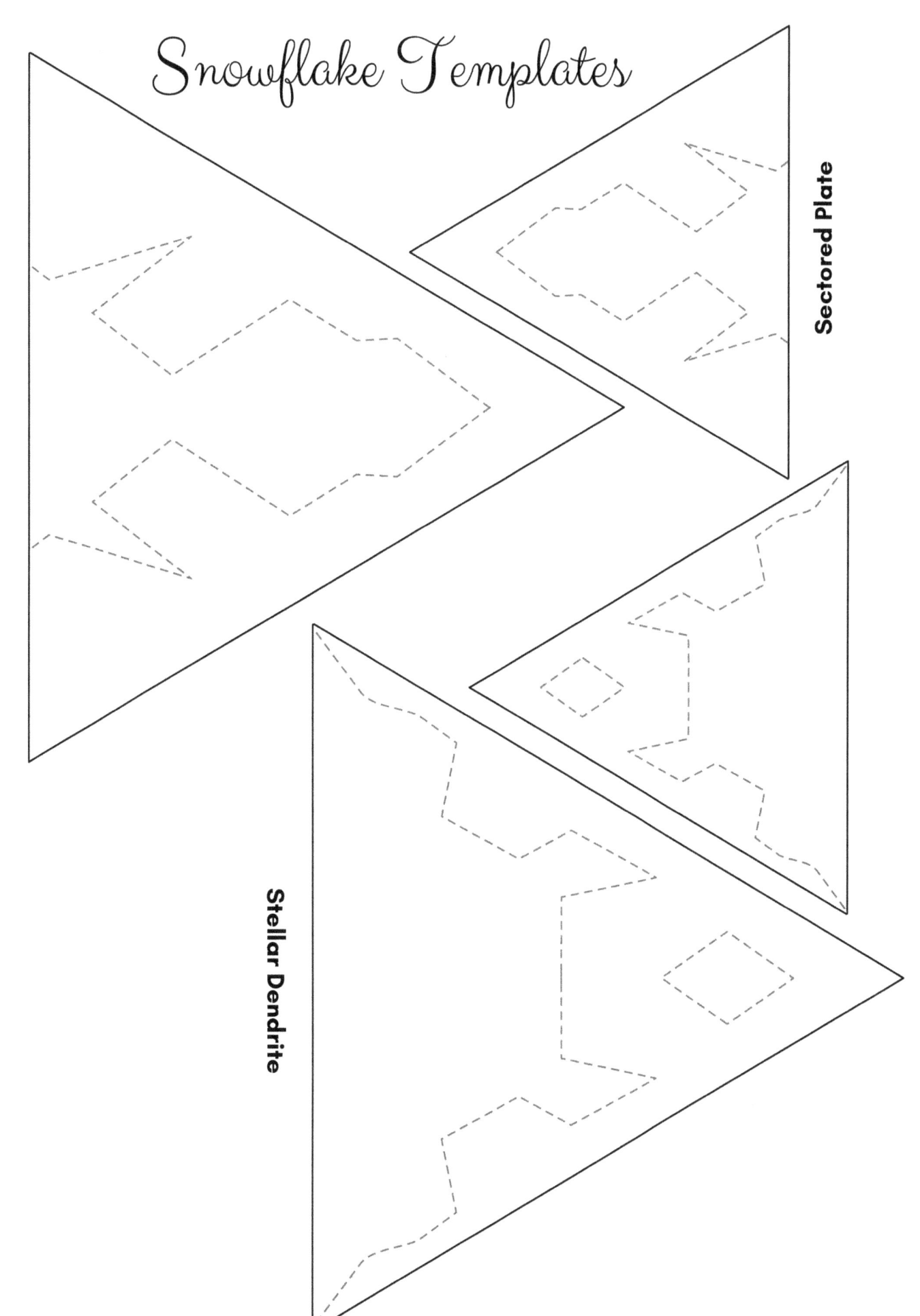

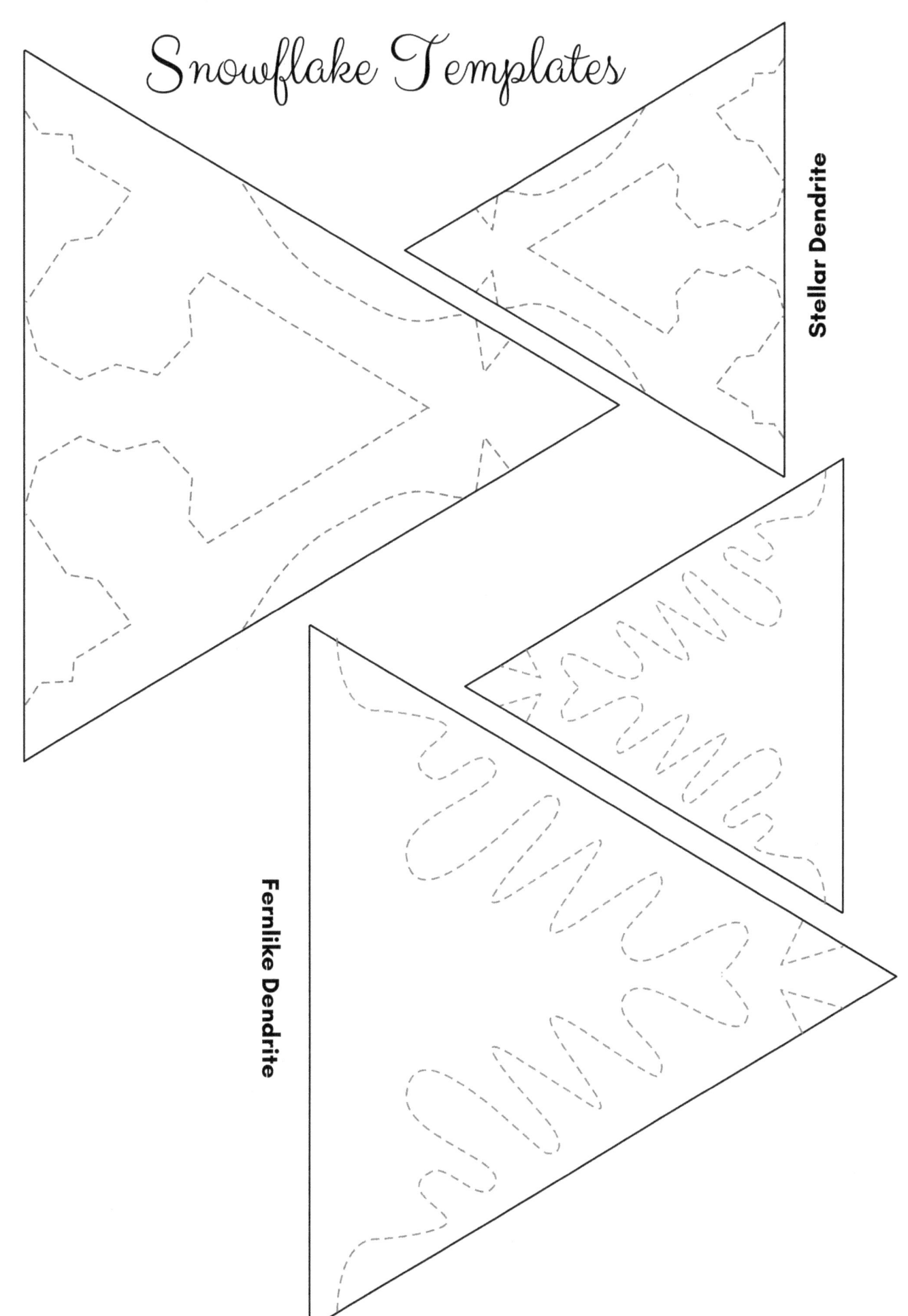

Snowflake Shape Labels

simple plate

stellar plate

sectored plate

stellar dendrite

stellar dendrite

fernlike dendrite

SALT SNOWFLAKES

Instructions

A snowflake forms when a water droplet freezes onto a small particle (pollen, dust, etc.) in the sky. As the ice crystal falls to the ground, water vapor freezes onto the primary crystal, adding to the crystal. Sodium chloride (salt) is also a type of crystal.

Locate snowflake templates. Carefully trace the lines with craft glue. The more detail with the glue, the more detailed the final product will be. Saturate the glue outline with salt and carefully slide off excess. Note: since the salt absorbs the moisture in the glue, it is most effective to complete one design at a time to maximize detail. Once all designs are completed, allow to dry completely.

Use watercolors or watered down acrylic paint to dab the tops of the salt to colorize. Be careful when dabbing with paint as its very easy to damage the glued salt lines. Once completely colorized, allow to dry again and display.

Materials
- Snowflake Templates
- Craft Glue
- Salt
- Water Colors (or Acrylic Paint)
- Water
- Paint Brush

Snowflake Templates

Snowflake Templates

Savy Activities

Travel the world through the interactive learning activities of **Savy Activities**; these hands-on resources provide parents, caregivers and educators practical ways to teach children about the world around them. Each book features a country, location or time period where subjects such as geography, history, vocabulary, reading, language, science, mathematics, music and art come alive by engaging auditory, visual and kinesthetic learning styles.

All activity books include geography with applicable maps, landmarks and locations. Historical events and time periods are visually represented with full color posters and flashcards, if applicable. Each book includes a set of fun-fact cards, poster and flag, if applicable. Paper models allow children to create 3D creations of major landmarks and structures. All books include a life cycle and anatomy of a plant, animal or organic compound, with flashcards and 3-part cards featuring important structures applicable to the theme.

Children learn scientific principles through active experiments and activities. Traditional customs, festivals, toys, clothing and art are also explored. Each book includes an exclusive themed mini-story featuring historical events or traditional mythology and folklore to promote vocabulary and reading. Where applicable, world languages are introduced through engaging flashcards, posters and tracing work. Each country has been meticulously researched by interviewing native persons and/or personal travel experiences to ensure the authentic culture is fully explored.

Savy Activities utilizes concepts from multiple educational methods to create unique resources allowing children a tangible and enjoyable way to explore their world. The **Savy Activities** series should not be viewed as a curriculum, but rather complimentary thematic resources to enhance traditional education. Because the individual needs and knowledge of children varies within standardized grade levels, **Savy Activities** resources have the flexibility to be used with preschool learners through early to mid-elementary years. For younger learners, adult supervision and/or assistance may be needed and activities presented in a simplified version. For older learners, resources may be paired with additional content from other materials to meet learning outcomes.

Check out our other products and resources at **www.SavyActivities.com**

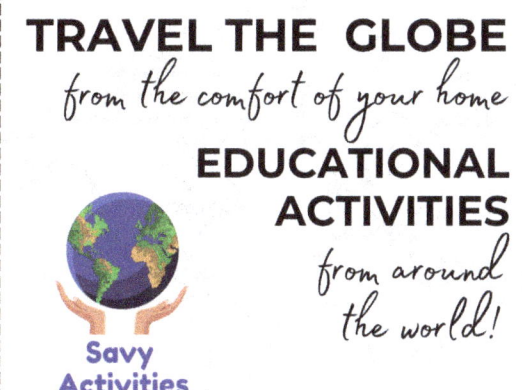

www.ingramcontent.com/pod-product-compliance
Lightning Source LLC
Chambersburg PA
CBHW060745240426
43665CB00054B/2994